Teaching the Child Rider

Teaching the Child Rider

PAMELA ROBERTS

J. A. ALLEN · LONDON

British Library Cataloguing in Publication Data
A catalogue record for this book is available from the British Library

ISBN 0.85131.794.4

First published in 1968 by J.A. Allen & Co Ltd
Reprinted 1973, 1976, 1981
Revised 1987
Reprinted 1991

Second revised edition 2000

Published in Great Britain by
J.A. Allen an imprint of Robert Hale Ltd
Clerkenwell House
45–47 Clerkenwell Green
London EC1R 0HT

Design by Paul Saunders
Photographs by Bob Langrish
Line illustrations by Maggie Raynor

Typesetting by Textype Typesetters, Cambridge
Colour separation by Tenon & Polert Colour Scanning Ltd.
Printed by Kyodo Printing Co. (S'pore) PTE Ltd.

In teaching riding, too much stress cannot be laid on the importance of a good beginning. From the earliest stages pupils should have the utmost confidence in their instructors, their horses, and their surroundings, and it is the instructor's job to inspire them with this confidence.

LT. COL. J. E. ('JACK') HANCE *School for Horse and Rider*

CONTENTS

ACKNOWLEDGEMENT

Photographs in this book were taken at Huntersfield Farm Riding Centre, Banstead, Surrey, by kind permission of the proprietors, Mr. and Mrs. David Horley. Their co-operation is greatly appreciated by the author and publishers.

INTRODUCTION

EACH YEAR many thousands of children start learning to ride. By far the greatest pleasure and satisfaction can be had from riding if it is learnt under instruction rather than picked up casually, for good habits and a sound basis formed in the early stages stand the rider in good stead later in his or her riding career.

Teaching of any kind must be a matter of both theory and experience. There are available to those beginning a career as riding instructors some first-class opportunities for training. In Britain, both the British Horse Society and the Association of British Riding Schools have systems of training leading to professional qualifications, and similar systems operate in other countries. These provide for the instructors a means of measuring their progress in their careers and for the pupils and/or pupils' parents some idea of the standards achieved by their teachers. Instructing, like many other human activities, is very far from being merely a matter of passing examinations, however, and there are many highly capable instructors who, for one reason or another, do not have formal qualifications.

Teaching children is a somewhat different matter from instructing adult novices and more experienced riders. Many who teach children to ride have developed their own methods, or variations upon more or less standard methods, in years of experience of this particular work. When dealing with children there are many special considerations regarding their physique and temperament which make teaching them to ride a highly interesting and rewarding task. Having had considerable experience of this fascinating work, I am very conscious that it is a sphere of riding instruction in which, like others, there is a tremendous amount to be learnt; in which, in fact, it is likely that more can always be learnt by experiment and practice throughout the instructor's teaching life.

A number of hints on the specialised problems and considerations involved in teaching the child rider are set out in this book, based upon the personal experience of friends and myself.

This books is intended to be of some interest and help to three main categories of reader:

1. The trainee riding instructor whose teaching practice has not yet included a great deal of work with children.

2. The parent in a horse-owning family who, although a competent rider, has little or no teaching experience and wishes to begin teaching his or her own child.

3. The non-horsy parent who wishes to know something of what is involved when children are sent to a riding school for instruction.

CHAPTER 1

PRELIMINARY CONSIDERATIONS

Type of Horse or Pony

THE CHOICE of a suitable horse or pony on which to begin to teach a child to ride – or of several suitable animals in the case of a riding school – is a most important matter and by no means easy. The age and size of the child or children to be taught have considerable bearing upon this, of course, but it does not follow that a very small pony is necessarily the most suitable mount for the small beginner.

To be really satisfactory for the purpose, the animal needs to be quiet and sensible but free-going, reasonably responsive but not too sensitive (as there are inevitably many involuntary movements by the novice rider), and to have good manners. All these qualities are not found frequently in young animals and a mature one is usually a more practical proposition. The animal should have reasonably good conformation and smooth paces. It should be fairly narrow, but not so narrow that its legs are too close together. It should go well in a snaffle bridle.

Opinions differ about the size of animal most suited to the child beginner, but in my view it is best to err on the side of one which is too large for the child. It is obviously ludicrous and totally impractical to put a small novice child up on a 16 hands (162 cm) horse, but within reasonable limits it is often best to teach children on larger ponies or small horses, of a size which is bigger than would be desirable for an experienced child of the same size. This is especially true in riding schools where many children of different sizes and ages have to be taught.

There are two main reasons for this. Many small ponies have a short action which causes a lot of bumping about by the inexperienced child, and with which it is difficult, because of the rapid sequence of steps, for the novice child to keep in rhythm. Even more important, perhaps, is the question of discipline for the animal. Horses and ponies ridden regularly by novices easily develop bad habits and are best ridden at fairly frequent intervals by experienced riders who can undertake any reschooling or revisionary work necessary to restore good behaviour and a satisfactory way of going. It is often very difficult to have really experienced small children available who are capable of doing this necessary work on a pony too small to carry the weight of an adult or older experienced child. Some very small ponies (possibly because they are extremely intelligent) are cunning and quick to take advantage of a small, inexperienced child. Often (though by no means always) larger ponies and horses are inclined to be more generous.

Very tiny children, whose introduction to the sport is to consist of being led about, principally at the walk, on a leading rein to get accustomed to the idea of contact with ponies, can with success be put upon tiny ponies which are then led by an adult. But such activity scarcely comes within the scope of the serious teaching of riding.

Provided the animal is narrow and has smooth action, ponies from about 13 hands (132 cm) to small horses of around 15 hands (152 cm) or so, according to the age and size of the child, are, in my experience, the most practical proposition for teaching children.

Tack

Necessary tack, apart from a snaffle bridle, includes a good, central seat saddle, stirrup leathers capable of being adjusted to fit short legs (it is a simple matter to punch additional holes if required, but long leathers used for small children result in a lot of unnecessary spare leather, which is inconvenient and bulky) and irons small enough for the child's foot, with adequate clearance for safety in the event of mishap. It is very dangerous to attempt to teach child riders using stirrup irons which are too big, as the child's foot can readily slide right through the iron, which can then run up the leg and cause serious trouble in the case of a tumble. A neck strap is an essential piece of equipment. A stirrup leather with the loose end secured by a leather runner or elastic band, or a strip of webbing about the width of a stirrup leather, make suitable neck straps, if that from a martingale is not available. The strap should be adjusted so as to permit the rider to hold it without bending forward. If the pony is likely to put its head down, the neck strap needs to be secured by side links to the front Ds of the saddle. Alternatively, grass reins may be fitted to prevent this. A leading rein is also necessary.

Teaching Facilities

Facilities which are desirable for teaching include a school or enclosed manège, permanent or improvised (a size equivalent to a standard dressage arena – 40 x 20 metres – is convenient but variations are quite practical and a somewhat smaller size is useful for very small children and small ponies), and quiet roads or paths nearby for use when working outside is undertaken. It is, of course, very helpful if a flat, well surfaced field is available. Useful equipment includes plastic cones for marking out the manège, a few simple poles and other materials for constructing small jumps, letters to mark the manège, if used, and one or two 'toys' such as old dusters, flags, buckets, balls, bean bags and the like for use in simple mounted games.

When small children are to ride ponies which are, strictly speaking, rather big for them, as outlined earlier, mounting can be quite a problem. A very useful piece of equipment is a specially made strong but portable mounting block which is light enough for a child to carry and which can be placed alongside the pony for the child to mount from. In my experience, although apt to cause amusement to strangers, such an aid is preferable to a fixed mounting block, as it encourages independence and prevents long waits to mount when several children are to ride at once. It is, naturally, essential to accustom the ponies to the use of the block before child beginners use it and to ensure that it is not readily knocked over, also, to make certain that the children stand in the middle of it and not on the edge. Plastic milk crates or similar flimsy structures, upturned buckets or feed bowls should not be used as mounting blocks. Any of these could collapse, slip or overturn.

Class Numbers

It is easiest to teach complete beginners individually, but if more than one absolute novice must be taught at a time it is necessary for the instructor to have one sensible helper to each pony. After the first few lessons, children learn more readily and more happily in company with other children, at least until an advanced stage is reached. As the instructor teaching young children needs, in any case, to have eyes in the back of his or her head, I have found it quite impossible to cope satisfactorily with more than six child beginners at a time. A class of from four to six is convenient, provided that adequate assistance is available in the initial stages.

Riding Wear for Children

Children grow out of their clothes very quickly and it is expensive and unnecessary for child beginners to be turned out as if for a fashionable show. Essentials for the child's equipment include a properly fitted riding hat which conforms to current safety specifications and is worn as recommended, with the chin-strap and harness always correctly fastened, and stout lace-up shoes with a good, sensible, low heel (or of course jodhpur boots if desired). It is quite a good plan to allow a child to have one or two initial lessons wearing well-fitted jeans or tracksuit bottoms (provided these are kept down by elastic or a strap under the foot) in order to avoid the expense of buying jodhpurs for a child who may not take to riding; but jodhpurs which fit well in the leg (even if turned up at the bottom to allow for lengthening),

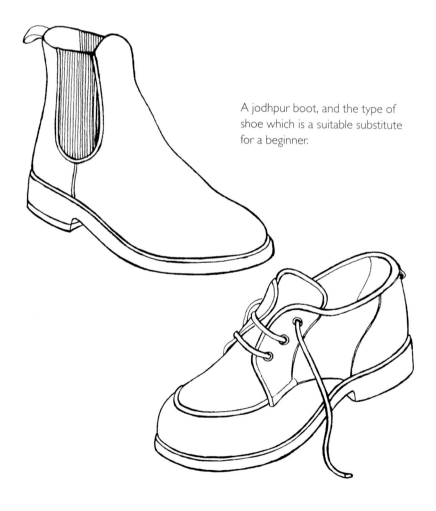

A jodhpur boot, and the type of shoe which is a suitable substitute for a beginner.

and have adequate room in the crutch, should be provided for the child as soon as it is apparent that he or she will like the lessons and before any vigorous work is undertaken.

The question of whether or not gloves should be worn is open to discussion, but if they are used they should be of non-slip material and should be well-fitted and not too thick. They should, of course, have fingers (i.e. *not* the mitten type of child's glove with a thumb and all the fingers in an unfeeling bag). Personally, I hate to see a child's bare hands becoming

Dressed for action, child and pony are ready for the lesson.

steadily more numb when riding in cold weather, or sensitive skin being chafed by the reins. It has, however, to be borne in mind that clumsy gloves are a hindrance and that if gloves are worn more or less constantly the hands are likely to chafe when they are left off. A sensible compromise is probably to wear them for lessons in cold weather and not when it is warmer. There will be times later in the riding life when the wearing of gloves is correct for proper turn-out, and it is sensible to become accustomed to their use at some time.

Pullovers, quilted or fleece jackets, bodywarmers or even anoraks (although these make it difficult for the instructor to check the child's position as they cause the rider to look rather like a blown-up pillow case if it is windy!) may be worn in lieu of a riding jacket. If a shirt is worn without an outer garment in warm weather, or under a sleeveless pullover or bodywarmer when it is colder, the shirt should always have long sleeves. These provide at least some degree of protection against scratches from brambles and branches, or superficial grazes in the event of a fall.

If the child rides in the rain, the wet weather coat worn to school can be used in default of a proper riding mackintosh. The bottom two fasteners should be left undone for mounting and dismounting, as they are liable otherwise to be torn off. On no account should the child be permitted to ride in a loose, light, plastic mac as these garments crackle, tear, flap and balloon in rough weather, with a real risk of upsetting the pony and causing trouble. A French pupil of mine once sought to ride carrying an opened umbrella, but while this is a hazard which has to be forbidden, I would think it a rare occurrence!

Children should not be allowed to ride wearing earrings. If caught on a twig or branch, these can tear the ear severely. If a child wears spectacles for riding these, as for other sports, should have lenses of plastic or shatter-proof glass.

Starting Age

Many people, particularly in horsy families, favour starting a child's riding life very early ('he was put up on a pony almost before he could walk'). It is seldom practical, however, to begin serious teaching before the age of about six. This can vary a year or so either way, dependent upon the child's mental and physical development, but serves as a rough guide.

While it is probably pleasant and quite useful for a child to 'sit on' and be led about before this age, this is usually only practical in pony-owning

…sought to ride carrying an opened umbrella.

families. Very little concrete progress is made before the age of about six. Moreover, when it comes to what might be called really active riding, with intelligence and purpose, little development in this sphere begins before about ten or twelve, except perhaps with children brought up in horsy circles and able to ride daily.

Child's Physique and Temperament

As with an adult, physique plays a part in progress and the slim, long-legged, naturally well-balanced child starts with a considerable physical advantage. Small, weak children, and those whose natural balance and ability to use their limbs independently are not yet well developed, present greater problems, but many of them benefit very considerably from regular and properly supervised riding lessons. Many children who, because of puppy fat, are like small barrels on short legs, also present something of a problem to the instructor, partly because they are quite literally top-heavy when mounted. But problems are there to be overcome and good progress is quite possible provided the teacher bears all such considerations in mind throughout all the work.

Children who are naturally athletic, and those whose other activities include such improvers of balance and muscular control as dancing or

It is probably pleasant and quite useful for young children to 'sit on' and be led about to get the feel of being on a pony, but very little serious teaching is practical before the age of about six. Here, two 'tinies' are enjoying a pony ride.

Physique plays an important part in progress. The long-legged, well-balanced child (above) starts with a considerable advantage over the child who is literally top-heavy when mounted.

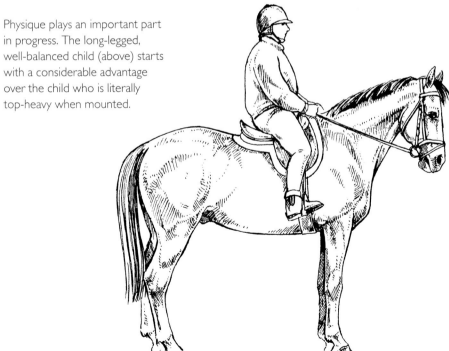

skating, are often easier to teach, from the purely physical aspect, than are others. But these children are by no means always those who have the advantage in what might be called the mental side of the activity. It is often easier to make real progress with intelligent, adaptable, determined children, and those with a natural sympathy with animals, who are not ideally suited to the sport by their physical conformation, than with those who are physically more suitable but less well equipped mentally for the work.

It is, therefore, most important for the instructor to study the physical and temperamental characteristics of each child pupil and to act accordingly. Teaching children, even more, perhaps, than teaching adult novices, is a highly individualistic matter.

Duration and Frequency of Lessons

Children, especially young children, tire easily when riding, although frequently they are not consciously aware of this themselves. Equally important, or more so, they become bored easily, too, or become mentally tired through excessive concentration. To many children, early riding lessons are unlike anything else in their daily experience and because of the newness and the physical effort and mental concentration required the lessons are quite strenuous for them, even when great care is taken.

It is, therefore, best for early lessons to be quite short — of say half-an-hour's duration. The more frequently lessons can be taken, the more rapid the progress made (provided always that rubbing and soreness is not allowed to develop), and daily lessons, initially of about half-an-hour each, are the ideal. With children from families who do not own ponies this is rarely practical, except where expense is an unimportant consideration. For children attending a riding school, lessons once or twice a week are suitable. A half-hour lesson weekly, in the early stages, is infinitely preferable to an hour's lesson fortnightly. Much is forgotten between lessons, and stiffness occurs more severely when the relevant muscles are used at infrequent intervals.

Where, for economic or other reasons, lessons are less frequent than is desirable, the instructor has to bear this in mind constantly to ensure that unreasonable demands are not made upon the child's muscles, or mind.

Choice of School

The choice of a suitable riding school can present the non-horsy parent with something of a problem. Choice is often inhibited by the availability of only one school within reasonable distance. Riding schools are listed in some local directories. In Great Britain it is a legal requirement for a riding establishment to be licensed by the local authority. It may be possible to obtain from the authority addresses of licensed establishments in its area. When choosing a riding school it is most important to ascertain that the establishment has a current licence. Apart from many other considerations, this is because the possession of the legally specified type of insurance cover is one of the requirements for eligibility for a licence. In countries where a licence is not required for the running of a riding establishment, it is important to enquire about an establishment's insurance cover. In any case it is necessary to realise that riding is a risk sport, and that even if the establishment is insured the policy can be expected to cover only legal liability (involving proof of negligence).

The fact that a riding establishment has a licence from the local authority is not relevant in indicating the standard of instruction provided, nor to whether or not it is particularly suited to the teaching of children. A booklet listing its approved establishments, and giving details of the facilities offered, may be purchased from the British Horse Society. The official handbook of the Association of British Riding Schools includes details of the association's approved schools and may be purchased from the association.

In making a choice of school, the availability of the facilities outlined earlier (Teaching Facilities) helps to some extent, and a school which caters specially for children is often preferable to one which does not. Personal recommendation from friends and neighbours is useful, but where this is not forthcoming the parent needs to look for a school where a responsible attitude is apparent, where adequate supervision appears to be provided, and where animals, tack and equipment appear to be in good condition. The availability of a qualified instructor or instructors is encouraging, but it does not always follow that such instructors are necessarily experienced specifically with children.

If reasonable progress is made, if the child enjoys the experience, and if it is obvious that great care is taken to guard against avoidable accidents, the choice has probably been a good one. The teaching of riding can be done satisfactorily in many different ways and is a subject about which dogmatism is quite out of place.

It might be, however, that some of the ideas expressed in this volume will serve as a rough guide to the parent inexperienced with horses about the *kind* of work and attitude which could reasonably be expected. It is most important to stress, however, that if activities are not carried out at a particular establishment in the order and manner outlined here, this by no means suggests that it is not an entirely satisfactory school for a child.

While it is fair to say, I think, that certain basic things are common to all good teaching of riding, excellent results are achieved safely and in a pleasant atmosphere by the use of a wide variety of individual methods.

CHAPTER 2

FIRST LESSON

Preparation

BEFORE BEGINNING the child's very first riding lesson, it is a good plan to find out, from a parent and not in the child's presence, any special characteristics or problems, physical or otherwise, which may affect the work.

Information is probably best obtained at the time of the initial booking when, naturally, the name, age, weight and height of the child will be ascertained, along with the parents' home address and telephone number.

The supplementary information which may be of value to the instructor includes such points as the child being used, or not used, to animals; being shy; having a weak ankle; being susceptible to cold; being able, or not able, to ride a bicycle (which gives some indication about balance – and possibly road sense) and a host of other matters which may on first thought appear irrelevant. The instructor will find however, in the course of experience, that points of this kind are extremely helpful in his or her work, when borne in mind intelligently. In consequence, many instructors will build up their own lists of such queries in the course of their work. Whatever else is discovered, it is extremely important to ascertain whether or not a young child knows left from right.

Before the start of the first lesson, the instructor should check that he or she has the child's name correctly. It is also important that the instructor explains his or her own role, and gives the name he or she wishes pupils to use if they should need to attract the instructor's attention. The simple human problem of communication is one of the most important items in the early stages.

Introducing the Pony

The child can then be shown the pony he or she is to ride, told its name, encouraged to have a close look at it and to speak to it, and shown how to pat its neck. It is important that the pony should be made to stand still and quiet while this initial introduction takes place. If any mild correction of the pony is necessary, this should be done quietly, calmly and firmly. Nervous children are easily frightened by sudden movements, and a sharp rebuke to a pony conjures up a quite unnecessary atmosphere of danger in the initial stages. In contrast, any tendency to roughness on the part of the bolder child should be checked at once, the child being made aware from the start that the pony is a living being, with feelings, and must be treated with consideration as well as firmness.

Mounting

The instructor can then show the child, by a clear personal demonstration (or demonstration by another child if the pony is too small for the instructor), exactly how to mount. This demonstration should be explained clearly, step by step, and may need repeating several times. The child is then told to mount and advised at each stage in doing so, as necessary. The portable mounting block mentioned in the first chapter may be used if the height of the pony and size of the child require this.

Common initial blunders are: putting the wrong foot in the stirrup, poking the toe into the pony, failing to hold the reins, lack of spring, and landing in the saddle with a bump. These, and any other errors, can be quietly corrected.

In my view it is not a good idea to lift the child, however small, on to the pony for even the earliest lessons (although a judicious boost under the seat may sometimes be inevitable if the child is very plump and lacking in spring and gets hopelessly stuck halfway up!). Mounting has in any case to be learnt at some time and might as well be taught at the outset. Moreover, nervous children are more scared if suddenly heaved up into a position of, to them, considerable height than if they have experienced some sensation of climbing, themselves, to get there.

A helper should hold the pony still while mounting is carried out. The helper can, with advantage, also pull down on the off-side stirrup as the child mounts, as early attempts at mounting are almost bound to be somewhat clumsy and it is wise to try to minimise the effects of pull on the

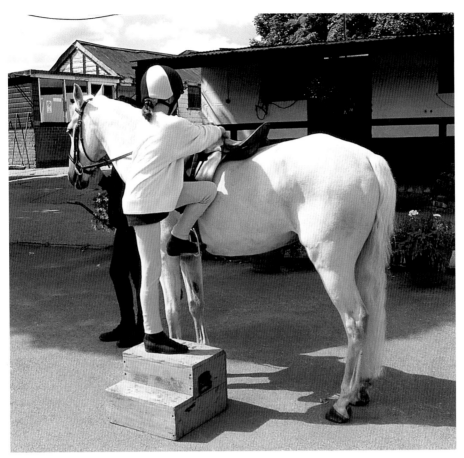

A beginner using a portable mounting block to mount a pony which is too tall for the child to reach from the ground.

saddle and the pony's back. Both helper and instructor should be fully on the alert while the child is first mounting, as they are quite likely to get kicked by the child's right foot, or have their fingers pinched while trying to help a foot into a stirrup, or be otherwise unexpectedly buffeted.

Adjusting the Stirrups

The stirrups can then be fitted. It is worthwhile expending considerable care on this. It is, of course, important to ensure that they are level. With very small children, or those with very short legs, this is not always easy to see. The instructor will need to stand straight in front of the pony and may have to bend down to look straight at the stirrup irons from a few paces distance. It is, of course, necessary to ensure that the pony is standing level. In the event of doubt about whether or not the stirrup leathers are both of the same length, the feet can be removed from the stirrups which can then be examined, hanging free, from the front or back. If there are insufficient holes to adjust the leathers short enough and it is inconvenient to punch more, they can be looped around the branches of the irons as a temporary expedient.

The instructor is shown looping the stirrup leather around the branch of the iron, as a temporary expedient to shorten the leather more than the number of holes will permit.

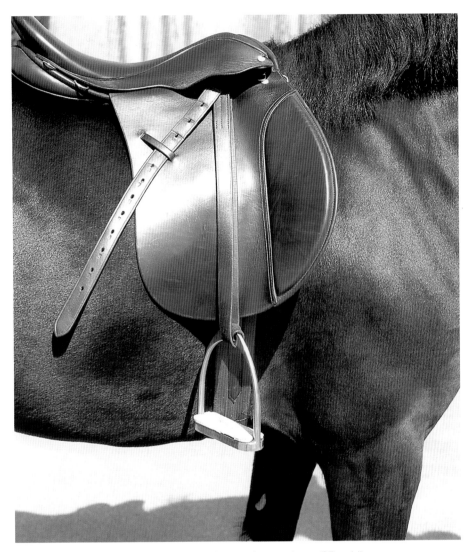

The finished loop is pictured here. Note the good, central seat GP saddle.

I have found it best to fit the stirrups shorter for the earliest lessons than would be desirable from the viewpoint of a truly correct position, since the child's muscles are unaccustomed to riding and the legs will inevitably be somewhat drawn up to begin with. If fitted at a 'correct' length, the stirrups will be lost frequently at first and the child will feel stretched, insecure and uncomfortable. Another reason for fitting the stirrups somewhat short is that the child will need much more support from them in learning to rise to the trot than is necessary, or desirable, at a later stage.

In order to fit the stirrups correctly it will have been necessary to put the child's seat in approximately the right place in the saddle and to have adjusted the position of the legs and feet. Personally, I start with the child's feet right home in the stirrups for the earlier lessons, as I think it is asking too much to expect young beginners to be able to keep them on the balls of the feet in the early stages, and attempts to insist upon this only result in the stirrups being lost very frequently, or encourage pressing down incorrectly upon the toes.

Basic Seat

Next the pupil can be shown how to sit, with emphasis on sitting up straight and looking ahead.

When showing the child how to hold the reins it is important to emphasise from the outset that they are for guiding the pony — *not* for holding on by. It should be explained that, if he or she wishes to hold something, the neck strap is there for that purpose, but it should be made clear that it is the legs, seat and upturned toes which are the proper means for keeping the rider in the correct position.

A common fault among children is to seek to hold the reins 'upside down' (the rein coming into the top of the hand between thumb and forefinger and out at the bottom). This appears at first to be a more natural method and many children will revert to it, often unintentionally, quite frequently during their early lessons. They must be constantly corrected about this fault if it occurs, as it is a habit difficult to eradicate if it becomes established and one which will be reverted to quite often in times of difficulty if not checked from the outset.

In many high-class establishments adults are taught initially on a lunge line, with excellent results. Older child beginners can be taught in this way. In my view, however, this method is not the most suitable for the initial instruction of the younger children, though such work is sometimes carried out effectively at a later stage. Children are often less well balanced and less able to control their limbs than are adults, frequently scare more easily, and are less easy to instruct in a way which requires logical co-operation from the pupil. Moreover, because they are light, they are less secure initially than older children or adult novices whose weight serves, to some extent, to keep them down on their horses. The instructor needs to have the child within easy reach for early lessons and the mount under very close control.

Early lessons for young children are best given on the leading rein. While

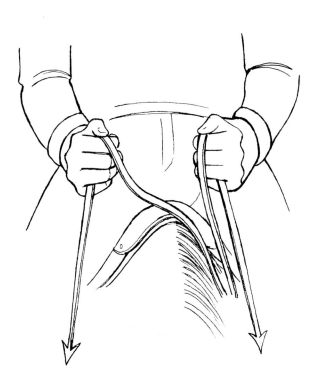

Holding the reins:
(above) correct method,
(below) incorrect method
often adopted by children.

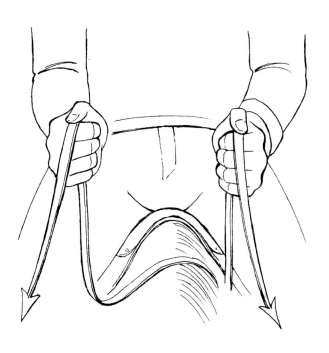

it may be quite practical to take an adult or older child out on a leading rein with the instructor mounted, for young children this is best done on foot. The earliest lessons are most easy to arrange under these circumstances in an enclosed space or manège.

It is extremely difficult to lead a pony satisfactorily at the same time as teaching the child. The most practical arrangement, I have found, is to have a sensible helper, experienced in the work, to lead the pony, while the instructor is free to walk beside the child and provide help as necessary. After one or two lessons, or several lessons, dependent on the progress made, it is possible for the instructor, standing in the manège, to teach several children at once, each being led by a helper on foot.

With a helper leading the pony, the instructor is able to walk alongside, steadying, helping and teaching the beginner.

Initial Movement

Having got the child seated in more or less the correct position and holding the reins correctly, it is time to introduce movement. This is a most important moment and the instructor should be fully aware of this fact, while not allowing this impression to be conveyed to the child.

When the unaccustomed sensation of movement of the pony is first experienced, the first lesson has reached the point when fright is most likely to occur, particularly in the case of the young child. The instructor has to plan carefully to get over this moment with the minimum of bother. So that the child shall not be taken by surprise, it is necessary to announce that the pony is now going to walk forwards.

It serves two purposes if the instructor first teaches the child how to 'ask' the pony to move, explaining that the animal is supposed to act in accordance with signals given by the rider. First, this introduces the idea of active control (rather than passengership) from the outset. Secondly, the child is less likely to be scared by movement which he or she feels has been personally initiated than by movement of the pony apparently without control.

The instructor therefore shows the child how to use the legs to squeeze or tap the pony's sides, the instructor's own hand pushing on one of the child's legs to indicate how it is to be used (the helper holding the pony still while this is done). The child can, with advantage, be told to lean slightly forward when the pony moves off as 'asked'. The child is then told to 'ask' the pony to walk forward, by using his or her legs – the helper leading the pony forward when this is done.

Many children, in 'asking' their pony to move forward, will flap the reins initially. This is an almost unconscious movement (born of 'gee up, Neddy' ideas of riding an imaginary horse in early childhood, perhaps?). It must be corrected by repetition of the information that the reins are for guiding the pony, the legs to make it go.

If this drill is gone through, the move off will most probably be made quite without incident. Some difficulty may be experienced, however; either the physical problem of balance or that of fright – sometimes both.

Balance

The first steps of the pony may cause the child's upper body to be thrown back to some extent and the hands to shoot up or clutch at the reins for support. Correction by the teacher will be necessary and some physical help, by gently pushing the child's body forward with the hand, may be required if balance has been badly upset. After the initial movement, this trouble will quickly be righted and most children can usually sit fairly comfortably on the walking pony. However, some children are naturally better balanced than others and while some can sit quietly on the pony, at least at the walk, from the outset, others are very wobbly. (Specific problems of balance at walk and trot are discussed more fully in the following chapter.)

Some wobbling may occur, particularly on turning corners (which should be taken wide and not sharply at first) and the instructor may require to steady the child with one hand, or gently push the body into position.

Fright

Fright can be shown in a variety of ways, from a look of tenseness or alarm to the extremes of tears or screaming. This last is not common, but is apt to be most disconcerting to the inexperienced instructor and it is wise to be prepared for it and not to panic.

Faced with a small child who cries or screams on first movement, I personally address him or her quietly and firmly by name, offering reassurance. If tears or screams persist for more than the first moment or so of movement I say firmly that by making 'that snuffling noise' or 'all that noise' he or she is likely to frighten the poor pony. This usually checks the flood, at which point a quick succession of quietly spoken instructions on where to look, how to hold the hands, the body position and so on, usually distracts attention until the first moment of fright has been forgotten.

If the screaming persists the pony can be stopped and the same procedure tried. I think it most unwise to take the child off the pony unless really serious panic has arisen – a very unusual occurrence indeed. A frightened child will sometimes demand to 'get down', but if removed at this stage from the back of the pony lasting difficulties may result. Such demands can be resisted by saying words to the effect of 'Oh, come on now, John, you don't want to get off and then have to go to all that bother to climb all the way up again, do you?'

Alternatively, the question 'Why?' (pursued if necessary) may suffice. The child can rarely put into words the reasons for the wish to 'get down', and the effort of trying to do so, which usually produces a snuffled 'I don't know', often distracts attention from initial fright.

If several young children are being taught at once, great care should be taken to see that they do not frighten one another. One child screaming may scare another who has hitherto been quite unconcerned, and several may consequently need calming at once. It sometimes helps to tell one child that he must be quiet or he 'will frighten Mary'. Alternatively a calm child may be held up as an example: 'Look. Mary's pony's moving too, but she isn't making all that noise.' 'You're too big a boy to cry. You're bigger than Mary', can be helpful too. I believe it is terribly important, however, not to *ridicule* fright or to humiliate one child in front of others for any display of fear.

Dismounting

When it is time to end the first lesson, dismounting must be taught. Although the child will have seen the instructor or helper dismount after the demonstration of mounting, and the teacher may or may not have explained how this is done at that time, it will have been forgotten by the end of the lesson. Since dismounting cannot be demonstrated on the pony which the child is riding and demonstration on another animal is time-consuming and often impractical, instructions for this have to be given clearly.

It is important to preface instruction on dismounting by some such command as 'Wait until I tell you', or 'Don't do anything yet; just listen', or the child is liable to carry out each movement as it is first explained and to dismount in a rush before the instructor is prepared for it. After instructions have been given clearly, the child can be told to dismount, each instruction being repeated individually as necessary.

The instructor needs to stand close and either help to ease the child to the ground by a hand on either side of the waist (from a tall pony) or steady the child upon landing (from a smaller one).

Almost invariably a child will stagger away from the pony on dismounting for the first few times, or may fail to get his or her undercarriage down at all. This may result either from lack of balance and co-ordination of movement, from the unfamiliarity of the manœuvre, or from the fact that the child's legs are stiff after riding. There is often difficulty in getting 'land legs' for a moment after unfamiliar movement. If the instructor is not prepared for this and does not steady as necessary, a tumble may result. The child may sit down abruptly on the ground (with the risk of back injury) on landing, or even, if very uncoordinated, take a nosedive and land prostrate. Such a mishap can be frightening, if not worse, and needs to be carefully guarded against.

Once on the ground, the pupil can be shown how to hold the pony, and

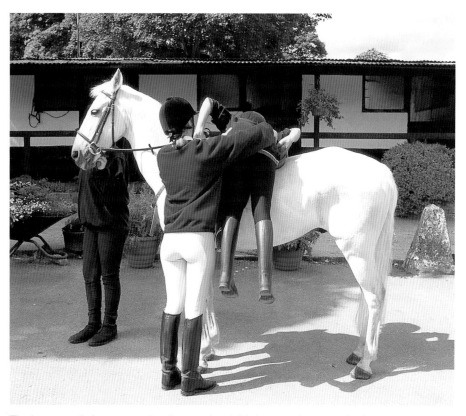

The instructor helps to ease the dismounting child down to the ground, with a hand on either side of the waist.

told not to let the reins loose until certain that someone has taken them over. He or she should also be encouraged to pat the pony in thanks for the ride.

Language and Content of First Lesson

In the first lesson, and, indeed, in all subsequent lessons, it is very necessary to try to ensure that the child understands all instructions. The instructor needs to be prepared for the necessity of finding words which the child understands.

While clearly I am not suggesting that the teacher should employ baby talk in teaching young children, it is very necessary to allow for the fact that the vocabulary of many young children is limited. The instructor should endeavour to select alternative words to express any meaning which seems unclear. At the same time it is a good idea to teach the necessary horsy terms, by clear explanation in other words as necessary, as they arise, right from the outset. For instance: 'Now you are going to *dismount* – that is, get off the pony'; 'Halt means Stop'; 'This strap, which holds the saddle on the pony's back, is called the girth'.

The content of the first lesson will vary considerably from child to child, according to how each pupil gets on. It will usually include, as well as mounting and dismounting, work at the walk, some effort at steering, stopping and starting. It may or may not include some brief periods at the trot, according to progress, and the age, strength and temperament of the pupil. The instructor will learn to gauge how much to attempt at the outset. In my view it is far better to err on the side of attempting too little than too much. It is important that the child should enjoy the experience, should not be frightened or strained in any way, should not be overtired and should be left eager for more at the conclusion.

CHAPTER 3

EARLY LESSONS

Walk

MUCH OF the work in the early lessons is carried out, naturally, at the walk. The child is gradually accustomed to being on the pony and a great deal of useful foundation work can be put in while walking. The basis of a good position in the saddle can be established by instruction. A good deal of repetition on such lines as keeping the seat in the deepest part of the saddle, the placing of the legs, feet and hands, is necessary because position is constantly lost during even slow movement at first.

A fairly common fault among children is to sit in a humped position and there is a tendency to look down at the ground. The idea of sitting up straight, so far as the upper body is concerned, is not always easy to convey. I have found it helpful to urge the child rider to 'grow taller'. Attempts to do this seem to produce the desired effect of straightening the spine and lifting the head and neck out of the shoulders. It is also helpful to try to induce the idea of stacking up the body like a pile of bricks – stacking the hips on top of the seat, the waist on the hips, the chest above the waist, the shoulders above the chest, the neck on the shoulders, and the head right at the top of the pile – and then trying to keep the pile together, beginning at the bottom and working upwards each time balance and body position are lost. This is a simile which seems to be readily understood by children.

It is important that the child should not be bored, and interest can be introduced into periods of walking by including practice in steering the pony and by the imparting of various pieces of relevant information such as the names of the parts of the horse and saddlery visible from the saddle without disturbing position.

A fairly common fault among children is to sit in a humped position and there is a tendency to look down at the ground.

It is useful to talk with the child about other things (school, brothers and sisters, hobbies and so forth) at intervals, so as to encourage relaxation and minimise tension. But care has to be taken with the talkative child that concentration on the work in hand is not lost for long periods.

Trot

When the instructor feels that some degree of balance and calmness has been achieved at the walk, short periods at trot can be begun. This will often be in the first lesson, but not necessarily if the child's temperament and/or balance do not appear to warrant it.

With children, particularly small children, the trot is inclined to disturb balance so much and can be so uncomfortable and bumpy initially that it is wise to attempt to teach the rising trot as soon as possible. The most satisfactory method is to begin with several short periods of slow trot (say the length of one long side of the manège – about 40 metres) to accustom the child to the feel of the action, and then to stop and teach the rising movements at the halt and afterwards in walk.

It is necessary to warn the child before trotting, indeed to encourage an active 'aid' from the pupil's legs, in a similar manner to that used in first moving off at the walk. Even so, balance will almost inevitably be lost backwards at first, with the hands flying up, and correction is necessary as outlined for first movement.

Before moving from trot to walk, which is best done before a corner or turn is reached, it is wise to tell the child to sit up, or grow taller, or balance will be lost forwards as the pony slows into walk.

When one or two short periods of trot have been gone through in this way, the instructor can explain that the pupil is now going to learn a way to make the trot more comfortable. With the pony stationary, the child can be instructed to stand up in the stirrups and sit down, holding on to the neck strap for support as necessary. At first the pupil will be able to do this only slowly, but the speed of rising can be gradually quickened by counting 'up, down; up, down' or 'one, two; one, two' increasingly quickly. This type of movement is extremely tiring for a child at first, and should be attempted for only short periods at a time, with rests between them.

It is extremely difficult to do a correct 'rising trot' movement at the halt, without the action of the trot to supply the movement, and the instructor should be content with what is in fact a standing-up-and-sitting-down movement. The intention is only to introduce the rhythm or timing. When the child is able to stand up in the stirrups and sit down again fairly rapidly for short spells at the halt, the same movements can be made at the walk.

Trot can then again be attempted, with the instructor counting the rhythm – 'one, two; one, two', or 'rise . . . rise . . . rise . . . rise'. Some children will get the rhythm of the rising trot quite quickly, with the instructor counting – even in the first lesson (although it will usually be found that it is lost almost immediately if counting is stopped). Others take a considerable number of lessons to begin to establish the timing of the movement. If great difficulty is experienced, repeated returns to practising the movements on the stationary pony will help. It is not necessary to worry if it takes some time to get the rhythm, as children who take a long time to learn this movement (which is really a matter of knack and co-ordination in the early stages) often begin rising rhythmically and well all at once when something eventually clicks.

It is usually best to get the child to hold the neck strap. One hand on it is often enough, but if the pupil is very wobbly both can be used. Otherwise a lot of uncomfortable pulling on the pony's mouth cannot be avoided at first. As balance and rhythm improve the child can be encouraged to let go of the neck strap for a few strides, taking it again if any unsteadiness becomes evident.

Common faults initially include rising too high; staying 'up' too long (almost forgetting to come 'down' at all); missing several 'beats'; clutching at the reins for support; losing the stirrups; pushing down on the toes; swaying from side to side; rising too upright; and being left violently behind the movement. The child should be encouraged to lean slightly more forward in the trot at first than is necessary for the experienced rider and the various faults must be quietly and repeatedly corrected.

In the early trotting lessons it is quite common for children to stick out their tongues (probably due to intense concentration). This should be watched for and corrected at once as a severely bitten tongue can result if a pony should stumble.

At first, it is much easier for the child to trot on straight lines. As progress is made, easy corners can be turned, but care has to be taken that balance is not lost on the curve. Small, light or badly balanced children readily slide outwards across the saddle on a turn or curve. They can be encouraged to push down on the inside stirrup, if this occurs. The instructor needs to be ready to pull the inside leg downwards, or merely place a hand on the knee to steady it, in the initial stages, if necessary.

Some children are very wobbly indeed in trot at first and a good deal of physical assistance of this kind needs to be given by the instructor until balance becomes gradually established.

I have taught children whom it was necessary quite literally to hold on the pony in trot to begin with, by a hand on the knee and even by pushing the shoulder of the toppling child, but this amount of assistance is not often required. The instructor should be ready to give it if necessary, however, as it is most unhelpful to allow the child to slide off at this stage if it can be avoided. With very wobbly children it is most important to maintain a steady pace, to give warning before trotting, to get them to sit up before moving from trot to walk, and to take great care in making turns and curves.

Basic Control and Steering

To encourage active riding right from the start, early lessons should include attempts at such elementary control of the pony as starting and stopping and simple steering. Asking for movement can be little more than pressure or

The instructor teaching three beginners in the school, each being led by a sensible helper.

taps from the legs at first, and stopping will be crude and achieved by pulling on the reins and/or sitting upright or slightly back. Steering will consist of pulling on one rein and using the opposite leg. It is premature to attempt any refinement of aids in the earliest stages, since the pupil will be unable to co-ordinate the different movements of hand, leg and weight to any great extent. It is important, however, to try to teach the child to give simple signals to the pony *firmly but not roughly*.

In all attempts at steering the pony it naturally helps greatly if the child is taught always to look where he or she wants to go. Riding in an enclosed space the pupil can be told to pick out some object, such as a tree or fence post, and look hard at it while riding towards it. Such simple manœuvres as turning across the school or down the centre, with changes of direction, can be attempted from the earliest lessons. The helper leading the pony should give the minimum assistance in steering, the child being encouraged from the outset to steer the pony actively as much as possible.

Common faults in steering include looking down at the ground in front of the pony, or at the hands, instead of ahead to the point to be reached, and pulling the reins outwards, with hands far apart, instead of in towards the tummy.

It will be found that most children are quite unable to use their limbs independently when riding at first. Using the legs will cause the hands to fly up; pulling on the reins will cause the legs to lose position (usually, but not always, forwards) and/or the body to overbalance forwards, resulting in the elbows travelling back behind the body. Attempts to use one leg alone will cause the other to move too, and the same, to a lesser extent, is true of one hand or arm. Corrections need to be given in all these and similar cases. These problems will be righted gradually with practice and various physical exercises, but some elements of difficulty of this kind will often remain until quite an advanced stage in the lessons, recurring at intervals as more difficult work is undertaken.

Practice in shortening and lengthening the reins can be carried out at the walk until this becomes a simple matter. Once this is learnt, however, care has to be taken that the child is not constantly fidgeting with the reins in the early lessons. A frequent error is to gather up the reins too tightly at every change of pace or direction. If not checked, this can result in producing

Three beginners are led by helpers in a turn across the school, side by side. The instructor is placed so as to be able to see all the pupils.

ultimately the kind of rider for whom, in the more advanced stages of riding, no horse will go quietly.

The Role of Parents

When a child is taught at a riding school or otherwise by some person who is not a family member, the question will most probably arise as to whether or not parents should be present during the lesson. In the case of very young, nervous children who completely refuse to be parted from a parent in unusual circumstances, there is really no alternative to this. Where there can be choice in the matter, I have found that lessons are usually much more satisfactory if parents are not present, at least in the early stages.

Some non-riding parents are worried by the sight of what appear to them to be the abnormal difficulties experienced by the child and it is hard to keep this concern from the pupil. Parents who have ridden for years may feel impatient at seeming lack of progress. It is also extremely difficult for some parents to refrain from attempts to assist or correct the child, causing loss of concentration on the pupil's part – and sometimes also on the part of the teacher.

Moreover, self-conscious children are very inclined to play to the gallery and even where this is not a problem a child will often look towards a parent for approval or sympathy (or merely to ensure the parent's continuing presence!). This is very disturbing to concentration and can sometimes have most unfortunate results if the child ceases to concentrate on riding or is not paying attention to the instructions of the teacher.

Since young children are usually brought by parents for their lessons and it is not always convenient for the adult to go away and return in time to take the child home afterwards, it is helpful to provide a place where the parent can sit in comfort (perhaps supplied with some magazines), out of sight of the child during the lesson. It is, of course, necessary to obtain the co-operation and understanding of parents by a clear explanation of the reasons for suggesting such an arrangement for the good of the child's progress.

It is natural that parents should wish to see how their child is progressing and this can best be achieved, if desired, by arranging for the parent to watch the closing stages of the lesson only. Since the teacher will naturally attempt to finish each lesson with something done well, and is unlikely to attempt to introduce something completely new at the end of a lesson, this time is usually the most convenient from several points of view.

Many parents wish to do something to help the progress of the child's riding lessons. It seems to me that the best way in which non-riding parents can do this is by carrying out at home such homework as the instructor may suggest. According to circumstances, this may perhaps consist of ensuring that the young child knows right from left – so automatically that there is no hesitation about this in the unusual circumstances of early riding; supervising the carrying out of any simple off-the-horse physical exercises recommended by the teacher; checking carefully, and reporting on, any undue stiffness, soreness or distress (especially any early signs of rubbing of the skin); ensuring that the child is carefully drilled in road practice and the need for good manners in riding as at all other times (as these things, too, are apt to slip under the stress of a strange new activity).

Parents can play a very important part, too, in backing up any reasonable discipline imposed by the riding instructor, for good discipline is very important in riding lessons if unnecessary difficulties and accidents are to be avoided.

Parents can help greatly when older children reach a more advanced stage in their riding lessons by providing, where they are in a position to do so, any books, visits or equipment *recommended by the instructor*. (It is most confusing to the younger child beginner if books or other instructional material contradict – or appear to contradict – what is being learnt at the riding school, or introduce ideas which are too advanced for the current stage of development.)

CHAPTER 4

CONSIDERATIONS FOR PROGRESS

Physical Exercises

TO HELP co-ordination of movement and to develop the muscles to be used in riding, a number of mounted exercises can be carried out. These can be introduced at a very early stage. They serve the additional purpose of supplying variety in the lesson and thus minimising the risk of boredom.

The type of exercise used depends to some extent upon the physical characteristics and bearing of the individual child and upon any special difficulties encountered in the riding. Of course, experience will help the instructor to select appropriate exercises for use in specific cases. Specialised exercises are a subject in themselves and can scarcely be outlined in detail here. Training from experts in this sphere can be of advantage to a riding instructor who encounters particular physical problems in his or her pupils. In general terms, however, the choice of exercises is a matter of common sense.

Apart from special exercises for pupils suffering from some definite disability, they fall into three main categories:

1. Those designed to help co-ordination of movement and the independent use of individual parts of the body.

2. Those to reduce stiffness and encourage suppleness.

3. Those designed to strengthen muscles and/or reduce *excessive* suppleness.

Almost without exception all pupils require exercises of the first type. Most require some of each of the second and third types, stiffness being more common initially than excessive suppleness but muscle strengthening being commonly required in addition to increasing suppleness.

Great care needs to be taken whenever physical exercises are given (as in the ordinary riding) that the pupil is not tired unduly and that strains are avoided. In practice this means that only short periods of each exercise should be given; that careful watch is kept for signs of distress; and that rest periods should be given between each set of exercises.

Some very simple physical exercises are suggested here which can be carried out with virtually all reasonably fit children who are not suffering from any specific disability or injury. There are many others which can be learnt by a special study of the subject or invented by the instructor for particular purposes.

From a very early stage in the lessons, *short* periods of riding without stirrups *at the walk* can be given. The child should be encouraged to allow the legs to hang down limply and then, on command, to raise the toes so that the leg is to some extent braced. This serves the dual purpose of helping to get the seat down into the saddle and of strengthening the leg muscles. It will often be found that the stirrups have to be lengthened after riding without them, as the child is more down in the saddle and cramped legs have stretched to some extent.

Most of the exercises are best carried out at the halt, initially. When they have become easy, some of them may be carried out at the walk (and *at a much later stage* at other paces).

Circling the ankles (drawing circles with the toes) – with the feet out of the stirrups – is a useful suppling exercise. This should be carried out both outwards and inwards – with both feet at once and with each independently. In the latter case, in addition to suppling, this becomes an exercise in using the limbs independently.

Bending forward from the waist (hands on hips) until the nose touches the pony's crest and returning to the upright position is a useful exercise for suppling the upper body and strengthening the back muscles. Bending backwards from the waist until the shoulders touch the croup may be practised occasionally to test security.

Raising one arm above the head (other hand on hip) and touching the toe on the same side is also valuable. Naturally this should be done with each arm equally, unless more difficulty is experienced on one side, in which case it can be practised more frequently on the difficult side. Care has to be taken to see that the legs do not move and the pupil should be encouraged to press down on the heel on the side opposite to that on which the toe is being touched.

Raising both arms above the head, stretching them to the front, then outwards to the sides and then downwards is useful. Later variations include altering the sequence of movements and lifting the right arm above the head while the left is to the front, and so forth, thus helping in the independent use of the arms. It is necessary to check that the seat does not bump up and down in the saddle as the arms are swung.

Turning from the waist to left and right, keeping the upper body upright and the lower body and legs still, is useful. This can be done with the hands on hips or arms extended. Variations include turning to touch the croup with one hand or bending forward to try to reach the pony's ears.

Arm swinging backwards and forwards from the shoulders, and leg swinging backwards and forwards from the knee, separately, together, and 'one forward and one back', is also most helpful. Care has to be taken to see that the pony is not kicked in the process; and also, again, that the seat does not bounce in the saddle.

Simple physical exercises are useful for improving balance, suppleness and confidence, and add variety to the lessons. Here the children are turning at the waist, with arms outstretched.

As progress advances, some of the physical exercises, such as touching the toes, may be carried out on the move.

Legs can also be stretched outwards away from the pony. This is tiring and apt to cause strain if overdone, but is valuable in helping to stretch the muscles inside the thighs and to get the seat right down into the saddle.

Standing in the stirrups (hands on hips) and lowering the seat into the saddle again *slowly* and without a bump is extremely helpful for strengthening the muscles and increasing muscular control. This exercise, too, is inclined to be severe at first and should be carried out for only very short spells. Care has to be taken to see that the legs are kept still and the heels down, or the exercise has no value and may in fact be harmful. It will be found necessary for the child to lean forward somewhat to stand in the stirrups and at first balance while standing in this way will be difficult to achieve. To aid balance initially, the pupil may rest the hands lightly on the withers or crest, but this aid should be dispensed with as soon as possible.

A development from this exercise, which can be practised when the child has learnt the rhythm of the rising trot, is to give periods of rising trot performed without holding the reins or neck strap. For this exercise it is best for the arms to be folded. The correct way to fold the arms in riding is by holding the elbows with the cupped hands (rather than by tucking the hands through the arms), as the fold can be released at once in an emergency. The rising trot with folded arms is a useful exercise in balance and helps to teach independence of the seat from the reins.

The correct method of folding the arms for mounted exercises. The elbows should be cupped in the opposite hands as illustrated; the hands should not be tucked into the bends of the opposite elbow joints.

Other useful exercises which are also practical and help to achieve confidence and relaxation include riding with the reins in one hand for short periods, fishing out and using a handkerchief with the free hand, patting the pony's neck, removing and replacing a glove, undoing and doing up the coat buttons and any other simple tasks of this kind which help to increase dexterity and come in useful later.

Into this category comes altering the stirrups, which all pupils should be taught to do correctly for themselves as early as possible (although for a considerable time the instructor will need to check their correct adjustment and secure fastening). Practice should be given in doing this both at halt and on the move.

On the move (in walk initially), quitting the stirrups and taking them again without looking down should be practised. This not only increases muscular control, suppleness and agility, but saves a great deal of trouble later when stirrups are lost accidentally. At first the teacher will have to help the foot into the stirrup, but gradually, as lessons progress, the child will have learnt to fish about a little for the stirrup to find it and a very useful habit will have been established.

Another exercise which is useful in encouraging independent use of the limbs and dexterity – as well as being very valuable from a practical point of view – is mounting and dismounting from the off (right) side. Once the child has learned to mount and dismount well from the near (left) side, doing so from the off side may be required from time to time.

By way of encouraging independence, I usually leave it to pupils to discover the method of mounting from the 'wrong' side for themselves. In many cases, pupils will first put their left foot into the stirrup and begin to mount. Unobservant children sometimes even go so far as to land on the pony's back facing the tail and their surprise adds a welcome touch of

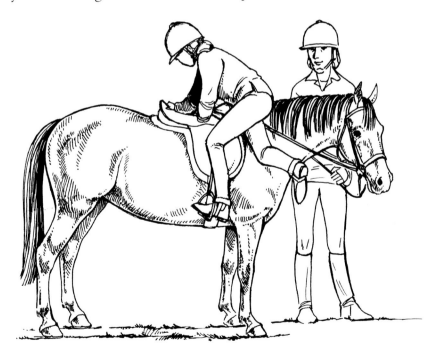

This can happen when a child is left to discover how to mount from the off side.

humour to the lesson! The helper should hold the pony's head low when this exercise is first attempted or it may be hit by the leg of a child going up back to front. When dismounting on the off side is first tried, the instructor should be ready to steady the child on landing, as in early lessons in dismounting on the near side.

A further useful exercise which may be practised is to teach the child to receive a leg-up correctly. Great care needs to be taken when doing this, as the child's co-ordination of movement will probably be poor in the early stages and the 'legger' may suffer back strain if unprepared.

If the child appears to be very stiff, some off-the-horse exercises can be suggested for practice at home. Ankle circling can be practised at any time. Arm movements and turning from the waist can be carried out while seated astride on a kitchen chair. Bending to touch the toes with alternate hands, with legs apart, helps to supple the back muscles. Head-rolling exercises are useful for suppling a stiff neck. Lengthening and shortening the reins can be practised with a dog's lead or similar substitute.

Twirling a pencil or stick across the hand, over and under the fingers, helps to supple the hands and increase dexterity. If the child has very turned-out toes, practising walking in a pigeon-toed manner is helpful.

The old-fashioned deportment idea of walking about for short periods with a book on the head helps to improve general carriage in the case of a child who rides hump-backed.

Of course, no physical exercises should be recommended for any child who suffers from a physical disability without medical advice.

Temperament and Concentration

The earliest lessons provide an excellent opportunity for the instructor to attempt to assess the temperament of each pupil. Knowledge of this gained in the early stages provides invaluable background for later work.

Is the pupil unduly nervous? Bold? Hesitant? Shy? Sensitive and imaginative? Slow or quick to learn or grasp instruction? Even- or quick-tempered? Active or lazy? Naturally inclined to be obedient or rebellious? Spurred on by difficulty, or easily discouraged? These, and other factors, such as a sense of humour, a competitive streak and (relative to age), a sense of responsibility, may be gradually discovered during the early lessons and have a considerable bearing upon the way in which later lessons are angled to achieve the best possible results.

Concentration is necessary if progress is to be made. Children tire easily when riding – both mentally and physically – and, particularly in the case of the younger ones, get bored easily too. It is best to arrange lessons so as to have short periods of concentrated activity interspersed with frequent periods of rest or change.

Discipline

Partly for safety reasons, partly so that progress can be made, and partly for the good of the instructor's blood pressure, it is very necessary that good discipline should be maintained during riding lessons. By this I do not mean that regimentation or undue strictness is necessary or desirable. Riding lessons should be interesting, enjoyable and fun for children. But, obviously, in a sport which involves the use of a living creature, has a considerable number of physical difficulties, and needs concentration, it is essential that the instructor should be able to achieve a reasonable measure of obedience from every pupil if accidents are to be avoided or complete chaos is not to result.

Young instructors, or those inexperienced with children, sometimes find more difficulty in this matter than in almost any other aspect of their work. It is necessary to make it clear, right from the outset, by an assured, firm but reasonable manner, that the instructor expects to be obeyed. In setting out with this attitude, the instructor should be mindful not to make unreasonable demands upon young pupils which would inevitably invite difficulty. A happy atmosphere of co-operation is necessary. Much the same attitude of mind as that required in schooling young horses is helpful in teaching children, provided that allowance is made for the greater intelligence of the latter.

Deliberate acts of indiscipline cannot be ignored, if respect is to be maintained. The instructor needs ingenuity to devise suitable punishment if necessary. In my experience this best consists of the withdrawal of something which the child enjoys (such as the privilege of watching a later lesson or seeing the pony eat its feed; or later in the lessons, 'no jumping today').

Acts of indiscipline involving discomfort to the pony can be corrected by making the child get off and walk! A short run round the school works wonders in curbing the exuberance of children who persistently treat the pony in a deliberately inconsiderate or rough manner.

In the event of serious disciplinary trouble arising, the instructor has available one decisive sanction. He or she can threaten to stop the lesson then and there – and be prepared to carry out the threat if necessary. A member of a class can be sent out while the remainder continue their lesson. A child can be taken home half-way through a hack-out (provided a responsible helper is available to do this in the case of a class). In a long experience of teaching children I have found that such a threat has actually to be carried out only very rarely – but seldom requires repeating if it is!

Actions of this kind need to be explained sensibly to parents. They are normally understanding about them when it is pointed out that discipline is essential for the child's own safety. But a riding school needs to be prepared to refund the money for a lesson curtailed in this way.

Pupils' Comfort and Well-being

Children, particularly young children, rarely complain when riding. They will often suffer all kinds of minor discomfort and sometimes actual pain, without drawing attention to it. The instructor needs to be constantly on the watch for signs of discomfort, fatigue or distress.

Much of this difficulty is no doubt caused by shyness, embarrassment, the strangeness of the unaccustomed activity of riding or an inability on the part of the child to express the problem clearly. Children will ride along sniffling in cold weather rather than take one hand off the reins to seek a hankie, or ask for help. They will suffer a rubbed leg, an itch, a gnat-bite, or feeling sick, in the same way. They will even sometimes endure cramp or a 'stitch' (a fairly common occurrence during early trotting lessons) without complaint. They will hardly ever ask to go to the toilet if uncomfortable while riding. They will sit upon rucked-up breeches or short-bodied ones which cut them in the crutch, in considerable discomfort, without comment. Sometimes they will endure silently some discomfort so intense that they are actually crying quietly while riding along.

The instructor needs to be constantly on the look-out for things of this kind, so that they can be put right *before* distress becomes severe.

It is useful when a class is stopped for rest specifically to *instruct* 'anyone who wants to go outside' to 'get off now, while we are resting'. With very small children, it is quite a good idea to insist that they visit the toilet before the lesson begins. Even so, the excitement of riding – and perhaps apprehension – can make a further visit necessary during the lesson.

Before, and if necessary during, the lesson the instructor should check that everything is in order with the child's equipment; especially that the skull cap fits properly and is worn correctly; and that clothing is not tight or cramping.

After the first few lessons – perhaps most suitably when the neck strap has no longer to be held for trotting – the pupil should be taught to carry a whip (although its correct use may be taught only at a considerably later stage, dependent upon circumstances). Children's riding whips are readily available. One with a domed knob on the head, to prevent its slipping through the hand, is preferable.

Many children's whips are supplied with a leather strap at the head end. The instructor should always ensure that the child has not got this abomination looped around a wrist to avoid dropping the whip. Carried in this way the whip can be most dangerous. Catching the end of the whip in a gate or branch, or some other projection, when the hand is through the whip loop can easily result in an injury to the wrist, or the child being pulled off the pony, or both. Countless dropped whips are preferable to these risks. Personally I try to persuade the parents to cut off the loop altogether if it gets in the way or if the child persists in putting a hand through it.

Riding out on the Leading Rein

Quite early in the lessons, children may be taken out on quiet roads or lanes to provide variety and interest. The rising trot is often developed more readily on straight lines than in the manège, with its constant cornering.

Grass reins are fitted to prevent this pony from putting its head down to eat grass.

Provided that the ponies are well behaved and the helpers experienced, several children may be taken out safely in charge of an instructor — each pony being on a leading rein. (It is helpful to fit grass reins to any pony which is liable to put its head down to eat grass when led out carrying a small beginner.) It is of course possible, and sometimes convenient, to take out several children on leading reins led from horses. In my experience it is greatly preferable, especially in the case of young children, to lead them from the ground as the helper is then readily at hand and free to give help really quickly if needed. This naturally limits the distance which can be covered and the length of periods of trotting (unless the instructor has a staff of first-class athletes!).

CHAPTER 5

SITTING TROT AND CANTER

Sitting Trot

WHEN THE child has learnt the rising trot, to the extent of being able to maintain the rising rhythm constantly on straight lines and around curves and corners without the necessity for the instructor to count the time, the sitting trot can be taught.

It is best to begin this by requiring (after an upward transition from walk) a few strides at sitting trot before rising is begun and again, a few strides at sitting trot before a downward transition to walk. There will naturally be a strong tendency for the pupil to bump in the saddle. The legs will most probably be drawn up at first and the toes will probably drop. It is quite likely that weight will be taken out of the stirrups and the stirrups lost. The upper body will probably jerk a good deal and the hands are almost sure to jerk the reins, and may fly up. There will be a lot to be corrected gradually. As in the earlier stages, the instructor may need to give physical help, particularly on corners, as the rider is likely to tip or slide outwards. Very small or light children are inclined to bump alarmingly at first, and short, plump children with short legs will be found to be definitely top-heavy. All should be encouraged to relax as much as possible, and to sit more upright than in rising trot. The various faults must be patiently corrected, as body and leg position will be lost frequently.

The work in sitting trot can be increased gradually, say by requiring sitting trot along the short sides of the manège with rising along the long sides. As balance improves, longer periods in sitting trot can be given, but it is important not to overdo this as the work is very tiring for the child and (initially) rather uncomfortable and disturbing for the pony.

Canter

It is quite a problem for the instructor to decide when to begin work at the canter, and this has to depend very much upon the progress of the individual child and upon other circumstances. In teaching adults or older children – especially if being taught initially on the lunge – it is possible to treat canter as 'just another pace' from the viewpoint of teaching the pupil to 'sit on'. However, this is not always so with small children: there is quite a big step from trot to canter in their case. At this stage, the teacher of the child rider may well, in fact, envy the instructor with an adult or older child on the lunge – but attempts to teach a small, young child beginner to canter on the lunge are fraught with difficulty, because there is a very strong tendency for the child to fly off the pony outwards on the circle.

There are, in fact, various difficulties inherent in teaching young children to canter. First, the small child, having little body weight and muscles not so developed by other sports as an older child or adult, is rather more likely to fall off at the faster, less 'flat', and 'lop-sided' pace (the trot, being a diagonal pace, although bumpy for the beginner, has the advantage of being, as it were, 'equal' on both sides and one set of diagonals has the effect of counteracting the sideways displacement of the rider caused by the other).

Secondly, ponies which have an extremely smooth, low, slow canter, into which they move with absolutely no jerk or rushing, and from which they can return to a steady, even trot without any roughness of stride (not only without any help from the rider, but despite involuntary movements by the rider), are not very common.

If, for reasons already outlined, it has been decided on balance to be best to teach the child on a pony which is somewhat on the large side, it is not at all easy to lead the cantering pony smoothly on foot, unless it can produce an extremely slow, rocking-horse canter beside which the helper can jog and the instructor can be close enough to the child to help as necessary. Leading the cantering pony from a horse, on the other hand, does not allow the instructor to be in a position to give much physical help if it is needed.

Having all these considerations in mind, unless a pony with suitable paces is available, it is often best to delay canter work until the child can ride fairly well off the leading rein at walk and trot, and is reasonably secure and well balanced in sitting trot, before adding a new pace to the work. This means that the introduction of the canter has to be delayed until a reasonable measure of independent control has been established, which may take some time.

First lessons in cantering are easier on straight lines than on curves. Unless the pony will move straight into a canter by voice command, and return smoothly and quickly to trot in the same way, it is not at all easy in practice to achieve this down the long side of a manège. (It is not reasonable to expect the beginner to be capable of applying correct aids for canter at first.)

Therefore, unless a paragon pony is available, it is often best to give the earliest cantering lessons in a suitable place, such as a soft-surfaced lane fenced on either side, where the pupil can ride behind a mounted instructor or helper. The instructor strikes off into a canter which is brisk enough to allow the pony behind to follow suit, but as steady and smooth as possible. In this situation the pony cannot pass the lead horse and its pace can thus be regulated. This is not the easiest of operations to carry out, since the pony will often start cantering, receive a yank in the mouth and return to trot, but practice helps to improve the instructor's ability to start cantering just vigorously enough to encourage the pony to strike off in pursuit, but not so briskly as to cause rushing or jerking the child rider too violently. In this as in all other aspects of teaching riding, it is naturally very helpful for the instructor to know the individual ponies' characteristics really well.

When first going into canter on a straight line, practical signals for the child beginner can be little more than to go into sitting trot, feel both reins to prevent the speed of trot being increased, use both legs quite strongly and lean slightly forwards. In addition to being told all this, the child should be instructed to try to sit down as in sitting trot. Correct aids can be taught later when canter on a curve is possible and when the child is able to sit on at canter without risk of falling off from the action of cantering itself.

If the canter is first tried in the manège, the instructor should be able to give physical help if necessary. If by the lane method, this is not possible, of course, and he or she will need to turn round in the saddle to keep the child in view and correct difficulties by advice (which needs to be given quite briskly and clearly to be heard over the sounds of at least two animals cantering, and to penetrate through the fog of tension which may have overtaken the child).

When moving into trot from canter it is most important to urge children to sit up, or the change of pace can be sufficiently unbalancing to cause them to fall off.

Small children experience a very strong feeling of action when first cantering. One tiny pupil of mine once summed this up by a cry of: 'Oooh! It's just like flying!'

Common faults at first include violent bumping in the saddle, losing the stirrups, getting left behind the movement with the hands flying up (or, in extreme cases, the whole body seeming to fly up into the air and to be travelling along above rather than on the pony – a most disconcerting sight from in front but by no means always followed by parting company with the pony completely), clutching at the reins for support, sitting very humped, drawing the legs up and attempting to grip with the heels, or turning the toes right out and gripping with the backs of the calves. All of these things require correction, of course, and the instructor has to try to encourage the child to relax and sit down as much as possible.

If any of the more violent upsets of balance outlined have occurred it is most important to try to return to trot as smoothly as possible, when it is decided to do so. Provided that the child has remained on top during the transition to canter, the most likely moment for falling off is on return to trot rather than during the canter itself, so the pupil should be encouraged to begin rising immediately on return to trot, if necessary by returning to a firm counting of 'rise . . . rise . . . rise'. It does not necessarily help much to return to trot at once if balance has been upset by strike-off into canter, for if a smooth canter can be maintained for a reasonable distance balance may be regained better than by again changing pace. Cantering should only be for reasonably short spells at first, of course, as the child will tire quickly.

Balance is usually much easier if the earliest canters are begun up a slight incline rather than on the flat and cantering down even the mildest dips should be avoided at first as these are most unbalancing.

The unaccustomed movements of canter often cause the child to forget what has been learnt previously, and the pupil should be reminded of the continuing need to steer and control the pony, and to try to maintain a correct position while cantering.

Some children, on first cantering, will drop one or both reins, possibly because they have been jerked from their hands during strike-off; perhaps because they have abandoned them in a moment of surprise at the movement, or to clutch the neck strap. When this happens it is helpful that the pony is hemmed in behind the instructor's horse.

It is very common for children to hold their breath when first cantering. If this happens they need actually to be told to breathe deeply and may even need be told to 'breathe in; breathe out' at intervals until this trouble has stopped. Some small children go almost blue in the face and are gasping for air at the end of a short canter, because of holding their breath. Various methods should be tried to get them to relax, such as encouraging them to sing, whistle or talk.

If children are frightened by the feel of the strange action when first cantering, they need, of course, to be reassured in the same way as in the earliest lessons.

When first introducing canter, as in introducing all other new movements, it is important to plan carefully and take all possible precautions to prevent the child from falling off simply as a result of the action, as distinct from some mistake or misbehaviour on the part of the pony.

After the first few lessons in cantering, efforts can be made to teach the child to sit down to the canter as much as possible. Exercises on the ground in swinging the seat forwards with the legs apart help to encourage this, but inevitably it will take some time before the pupil is able to sit down well. In the early stages the best that can be expected is that the child should be able to maintain a reasonable position and balance, without flying about too much, and should be able to maintain some reasonable control over the pony for short periods.

CHAPTER 6

OFF THE LEAD REIN

WHEN THE child is reasonably secure on the pony and has some idea of controlling it, the instructor has to decide upon the right moment to remove the leading rein.

Anyone who has ever experienced the peculiar sensation of a first drive alone without L-plates after passing the driving test gets some idea of what this may feel like to the child. But this sensation is modified by the fact that the instructor and helper are present.

The best moment for the first period off the leading rein is towards the end of a lesson when things are going well. In the manège it can be removed in the closing minutes of the lesson, the helper continuing to walk beside the pony to resume control if this should become necessary and the instructor being ready to give advice. Alternatively, the rein can be slipped off while walking quietly back to the stables after a ride out on the leading rein, with the helper at hand in the same way.

Quite quickly the periods off the lead can be increased, beginning halfway through the lesson, and so on, until the time when a lesson can be begun off the lead. It is sensible to have the helper at hand to walk beside the pony at first, in case things go wrong, when the lead can be quietly put back; and later to be available to go to the pony if there is difficulty, although not actually walking alongside. Gradually it becomes possible to dispense with a helper for each pony, as the child progresses enough to exercise reasonably efficient control in normal circumstances.

Continuing Supervision

For some reason which is rather difficult to understand, a large proportion of children learning to ride, including those who are most intelligent and display a good deal of responsibility and resourcefulness on the ground, seem to lose much of their normal common sense when riding, especially in the early stages. I have never been able to account for this completely to my own satisfaction, but conclude that it probably has something to do with the excitement of being on a pony, some degree of tenseness, concentration on the considerable physical difficulties involved at first, and the fact that riding is quite unlike any other activity in the child's fairly limited experience.

Whatever the reasons, the fact remains that many children seem to be extremely lacking in common sense during early riding lessons. They appear also to have much less sense of self-preservation than an adult has in the same circumstances.

All this manifests itself most noticeably during the early lessons off the leading rein and, in some children, continues for a long time after they have become quite adept in the purely physical side of the activity. As a result, children require a great deal of supervision – much more, in fact, than adults at the same stage in their riding lessons – so far as the common sense part of the work is concerned. The instructor has to anticipate the situations which arise constantly in normal riding, and give clear warning beforehand and advice about how to cope with them. Inexperienced instructors, on first dealing with children, will often find that they have to instruct the children in matters which seem so elementary that to mention them seems ridiculous.

So many things fall within this sphere of the work of the instructor teaching children that it is quite impossible to deal with even a small proportion of them. A few examples, however, may serve to illustrate the point. Once having accepted the idea of this kind of supervision, the instructor has gradually to build up a kind of sixth sense to warn of the type of details which need attention, and which also helps in the recognition of the point at which a child begins to exercise more thought when riding, making such detailed control gradually less necessary.

When riding in a class in a manège, for instance, one child may be told to trot on round the school and join the rear of the ride. In many cases the pupil will do this quite efficiently until the end of the exercise when, unless specifically instructed to walk in time, he or she will continue trotting until the last moment, when the pony pulls up with a jerk on meeting the rear of the ride or actually bumps into the rear of the horse in front, with attendant risks of being kicked or of treading on the heels of the horse at the rear of the ride.

Outside, a similar problem can arise on approaching a road junction. Children who are normally well drilled in road practice will fail to look both ways for traffic, notice traffic lights at red, or other vital details. They often fail to allow for the size of the pony and themselves when passing objects, giving insufficient clearance in gateways and other restricted spaces. One child pupil of mine actually rode straight into the posterior of an unsuspecting milkman who was bending over to remove a crate from his float (fortunately with no very serious consequences); and another stuck her foot into the open window of a stationary car! In fact, many children seem to expect the pony to steer itself, allowing for traffic and other obstructions and for the legs of the child sticking out beyond its sides. They will frequently ride so near the kerb on a road that the pony knocks its fetlocks against the stone, or trips up it. Several, having been warned against riding over slippery manhole covers if it can be avoided, will cheerfully skirt widely out round them into the middle of the road in the face of an oncoming pantechnicon, or stop so suddenly in front of such a cover that the ride behind concertinas.

I find it helpful to impress upon children, when they reach the stage of riding off the lead and are learning to control the pony that, while they are on its back, they are responsible for looking after it. Because the pony is supposed to act only as they direct, it is the child and not the pony who must look out for both of them. The establishment of the kind of partnership in which the rider knows when, and how much, to rely upon the pony's natural abilities to get them both out of trouble in certain situations comes much later, after it has become second nature to the child to direct operations in the normal course of events.

In negotiating a lane with overhanging branches, it is necessary actually to tell the children at first when to duck – or one is likely to be hit in the face or swept out of the saddle.

On one occasion I had to rescue a small boy from the branch of a tree, where he was suspended, unhurt, after this had happened. It is hard to say which of us was the more surprised – he on finding himself up a tree, or I on turning to see the riderless pony cantering towards me and the boy not on the ground but on high.

A child who drops something will often either not notice, or fail to mention this, resulting in someone having to go back (usually through deep mud) on foot to look for a lost whip or some other treasured possession.

An adult novice who becomes semi-dislodged as a result of some minor mishap will usually display considerable resourcefulness and determination in finding some way to hang on and clamber back if possible. Many children, in a similar situation, will either remain poised on the brink as it were,

In negotiating a lane with overhanging branches, it is necessary actually to tell the children when to duck . . .

without making any effort to redeem the situation (assuming that the pony is co-operative enough to allow them to do so – as many ponies used for teaching children are), or will merely let go and fall off when this could have been avoided, unless actually told what to do, or helped.

There are countless other simple situations which arise quite naturally in the course of normal riding where this kind of help has to be given for some time during the early lessons. Beyond these, of course, there is the necessity for clear instruction on what to do in the many minor emergencies which inevitably occur (such as a pony shying at a paper in the hedge).

Many children, when semi-dislodged, will remain poised on the brink, without making any effort to redeem the situation.

The instructor needs to be constantly on the alert to anticipate such things and deal with them before trouble develops, in much the same way as if riding an untrained youngster, with the added problem of the extra time needed to convey instructions to a child who has then to try to pass them on to the pony.

Good Manners

Probably for similar reasons of excitement, tension and unfamiliarity of the activity, children who are normally well-behaved and have been taught good manners will forget these completely during the early riding lessons. They will barge rudely in front of people, allow gates or branches to swing back on others, neglect to acknowledge a courtesy and fail to notice what is happening to other members of the ride or passers-by, unless specifically taught to display good manners in all things of this kind in the particular context of riding.

Improving the Seat

At about the time when the child has achieved sufficient balance and security to enable work off the lead to be undertaken, the moment is probably approaching when short periods of work without stirrups at sitting trot can be undertaken in the manège.

This is, of course, a most valuable exercise in improving balance and helping to get the seat down into the saddle. It should be undertaken for short periods only (say, once round the manège, to begin with, increasing this gradually), as it is tiring and apt to cause strain if overdone. The same problems of balance outlined for early work at sitting trot *with* stirrups arise and need to be dealt with in a similar manner. Corners and curves may cause sliding outwards across the saddle which, without the stirrups to minimise slipping, can result in a slide off the pony unless the instructor encourages the child to sit upright and to put weight on the inside heel in particular.

Work without stirrups is best done with the leathers crossed in front of the saddle, and care has to be taken to see that they are not hurting the child's thighs (the buckles can, of course, be pulled down to guard against this).

Some periods at sitting trot in which the feet are removed from the stirrups, left hanging, and then replaced after a few strides, are useful to teach the child to find the stirrups again if they are lost while riding at trot or canter.

When good progress has been made with work in sitting trot without stirrups, a few strides at rising trot can be attempted. This is useful in strengthening muscles and balance, but should only be done for very short periods, as it is a very severe exercise.

Usually, in the early stages, after periods of riding without stirrups, the leathers will require lengthening, as the legs stretch downwards more and the seat gets deeper in the saddle.

Once some efficiency has been established at work without stirrups it is quite common for a pupil to go through a stage in which the stirrups are lost frequently when they *are* used, through failure to put sufficient weight in them, the child drawing the legs up somewhat and putting all the weight on the seat. Periods of practice in trying to sink the weight into the heels, without pushing the seat out of the saddle, will be necessary.

About this time attempts can be made to ride with the stirrups on the balls of the feet, instead of right home. At first the stirrups will slip constantly, and care has to be taken that they are not retained in position on the balls of the feet by pushing down on the toes.

When the pupil is really secure in sitting trot without stirrups, and proficient in maintaining good balance and security in the saddle at canter, short periods in canter without stirrups may also be taught. This helps in encouraging the rider to sit down well at the canter, but should only be attempted when a position of fair security has been reached. The precise point will depend upon the progress of the individual child and to some extent upon the smoothness of the pony's canter.

As in first cantering lessons, the most unseating moments are at strike-off, on curves, and on returning to trot, and advice needs to be given about positioning the body well for the work – in particular on sitting up straight on returning to trot and on adjusting the balance if the seat slips across the saddle or the upper body tips sideways.

CHAPTER 7

BASIC STABLE MANAGEMENT

TO INCREASE confidence, to add interest to the lessons and for practical purposes it is a good idea to teach the child something about handling ponies and some elementary aspects of stable management. This can be done either in separate lessons or at the beginning and end of riding lessons.

What is taught will naturally depend upon the child's age, physique and progress, and also upon temperament.

From an early stage the pupil can be taught to hold a pony, not to let it loose unless someone has taken hold of the reins or lead rope, and how to lead it about. Such practical matters as tightening the girth and running up the stirrups could come next.

Children can also be taught how to put on and remove a headcollar or halter, how to tie a quick-release knot, and how to put on and remove ordinary tack. They should be taught how to lead a pony out of and into a loose box taking care to guard against knocks, to close gates and stable doors, and similar matters. They can also be shown how to fill up water buckets, tip feeds into the manger and, if wished, the use of the various items of grooming kit.

Most careful supervision is required whenever inexperienced children are handling ponies in any way. It has to be borne in mind that a child is not strong and may be easily knocked or pulled over. Care has to be taken that small feet are not trodden upon or the child otherwise hurt or frightened. A child who can control a pony quite well from the saddle is not necessarily physically capable of controlling the same pony on the ground and of course, young and inexperienced children should be allowed to handle only kind, sensible ponies, with good stable manners.

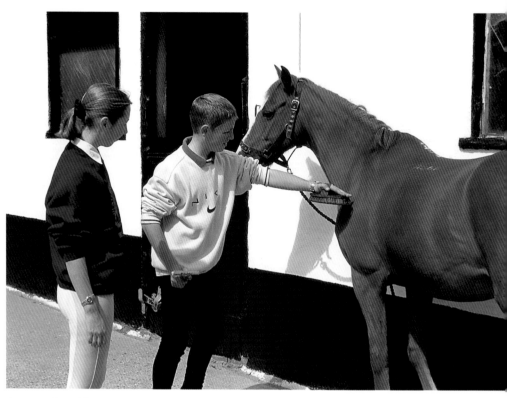

As part of a stable management lesson, the instructor is supervising the use of body brush and curry comb.

If children are to carry feeds and fill water buckets, suitably light equipment (such as a small polythene bucket) must be provided. As age and experience permit, a child who is interested in the work can be taught gradually all the normal routine of stable management, such as how to muck out, bandaging, rugging up and the like. However, it is important to see that the young and inexperienced child does not come into contact with anything unpleasant or frightening, such as the treatment of serious wounds.

It is also quite a good idea if parents give the instructor some guidance as to what the child has been taught about the different sex of animals, and like matters. Young children will inevitably and naturally wonder and ask questions about every new and interesting matter they notice or hear mentioned, and it is sensible to be prepared for this and to know how to answer the questions so as to satisfy the child, avoid embarrassment and not to create confusion by taking a different attitude from that adopted at home. In the absence of any guidance in this, I have found it best usually to answer

When learning stable management, inexperienced children should be allowed to deal only with kind, sensible animals. This boy is using a small, light, polythene bucket to carry water into the friendly piebald's box.

specific questions naturally and not to elaborate or add anything which has not been asked directly. The young or inexperienced instructor should be prepared for the likelihood of some surprising questions, otherwise it may not be the children who are confused!

However busy one may be, it is important to ensure that young children are not allowed to see or hear anything which might frighten or upset them concerning the routine of animal life, if this can be avoided. Nor should they be allowed to feel that something secretive or unpleasant is being kept from them.

When teaching children the elements of stable management and allowing them to handle the animals to some extent, it is most important to bear in mind that some have a natural aptitude for this and others have not. This is something which can be much improved with proper teaching and practice, but it is not possible entirely to provide the child with that indefinable presence or manner which is important. Some people have a natural ability to deal with animals and to know in some way more or less how they are feeling and what they will do. Others have not.

It is particularly noticeable when teaching children around stables that some, although untrained, have this quality or confidence (which enables them, for instance, to sense and check incipient misbehaviour even though their back is turned); while others seem always to be getting trapped in the corner of a box by a pony that normally has impeccable stable manners. The instructor needs to be constantly on the alert for this kind of thing if difficulties and accidents are to be avoided.

CHAPTER 8

Starting Jumping

Introducing the Basics

When the child is reasonably secure and confident in canter, a start can be made with some rudimentary jumping in the manège. The position for jumping is taught first at the halt, with practice in the necessary 'folding movements' of bending the upper body forward and returning to the upright position. These can then be practised on the move. Walking and trotting over poles on the ground, making the folding movement and holding the neck strap for each pole, can follow.

When this can be done quietly and well, tiny jumps – say around 1 ft (30 cm) in height – can be negotiated with the child holding the neck strap, first in trot, later in canter.

It is, of course, necessary to use a sensible, free-going pony with a smooth jump for this work, and it is often best for a lead to be given by another pony with an experienced rider, provided this does not cause the beginner's pony to rush.

Common faults which need to be gradually corrected include, naturally, getting left behind the movement, dropping the toes over the jump, losing the position of the legs, not 'folding' enough, coming upright too soon or staying in the 'folded' position too long, and looking down at the jump or ground instead of straight ahead. There may be a tendency to hang on to the pony's head too tightly, and this requires correction.

It is really important in the early jumping work to attempt only very small and straightforward jumps and to see that the child holds the neck strap until a good position and rhythm have been established – which may be quite soon, or may take months – dependent upon the individual child. If the child is not made to hold the neck strap there will inevitably be so much pulling on the reins at first that even the most amenable pony is likely to begin to stop or jump badly, making things very uncomfortable for the child, apart from the pony itself.

When a single obstacle can be negotiated well a second can be introduced elsewhere in the school and, later, a small double. As progress continues, further small jumps can be added until the child can negotiate a line of these in good rhythm and style. Work in a jumping lane, if available, can follow.

Throughout this work it is necessary to try to ensure that the pony maintains good impulsion so that uncomfortable, unseating jumps are avoided.

In due course jumping over tiny obstacles with reins knotted and folded arms can be introduced, and/or jumping without stirrups. It is important that only a very little work should be attempted at a time and slow and gradual progress aimed at to avoid strains and loss of confidence.

This girl, who has been riding for some time, negotiates a treble of small jumps. The instructor is walking beside the jumps, a little behind the small horse, encouraging it forward and instructing the rider.

An early jumping lesson. The pupil, holding the neck strap, is looking ahead to see the helper's gesture of putting a hand on the shoulder, and is concentrating on this rather than upon the tiny jump. The instructor is standing beside the jump, in a position to advise as necessary.

Jumping work is best carried out towards the end of the lesson when the pony is going freely and the child is down in the saddle as much as possible and riding to best effect.

Confidence

The most important part of the jumping work is the question of confidence. Inevitably many children will be apprehensive to some degree and it is the main task of the instructor to deal with this side of the work. Position and style can be developed gradually. Nerve, if once lost, is difficult to restore and great patience and care are necessary to see that jumping is enjoyable and that fright is avoided.

The best way of doing this – apart from proceeding only very slowly and gradually with the work – is to set the child various simple tasks to do while jumping. These can vary from watching a helper who is standing some way off on the landing side of the jump and being able to report on what gesture the helper has made during the jump (a clear one, such as raising one arm, for instance) so that the child is concentrating on what is ahead rather than bothering about the tiny obstacle, to more complicated tasks such as patting the pony's neck or tying a knot in a piece of string while going down a line of small jumps, in later stages.

A very good aid to relaxation is to get the child to sing or whistle while approaching, crossing and riding on after the jump (or, for that matter, at any other time when nerves are a problem). If a pupil is unable to sing or whistle, reciting a nursery rhyme or poem will do instead. The instructor can urge that any other members of the class should be able to hear the singing ('We can't hear you . . . we *still* can't hear you – sing a bit louder . . . louder still' – by which time the jump has long passed behind) and a small contest can even be run to see who can sing or recite the loudest and clearest.

There are all sorts of tasks of this kind which the instructor can devise with ingenuity and, provided that they are not so difficult as to upset balance, they can do nothing but good in distracting attention from any apprehension felt by the nervous child.

Falls

Almost inevitably at some time during the jumping lessons – and at other times during riding – there will be some falls; by far the most common of these being a fall of the rider from the pony, rather than a fall by both.

Especially in the earlier stages, the instructor will of course take all possible precautions to avoid falls.

These precautions include:

1. Introducing new work only when the pupil is ready for it.

2. Trying to avoid situations which provoke difficulty.

3. Ensuring that all equipment used is as safe as possible and that jumps are small, easily negotiated by the pony and not so placed as to be difficult.

4. Ensuring that jumps are so constructed and sited that there is the minimum risk of injury if a fall occurs.

If these precautions are taken it should be most uncommon for a fall to result in any serious physical harm to the child, but any fall, however innocuous, can be frightening and could damage nerve.

If, despite all reasonable care, a child falls off, the instructor should treat the incident as lightly as possible. A hard-hearted attitude is certainly not necessary, and may be quite harmful, but the minimum fuss should be made. If, as is most likely, the child immediately gets up after the fall and has plainly fallen without damage, the whole thing can be treated quite jocularly on 'Why did you go and do a thing like that?' or 'I didn't ask you to get off just yet' lines, and the child can be helped to catch the pony, popped back on and the work resumed as speedily as possible.

If the child fell heavily, is winded or badly frightened, it is not a good idea to act too precipitately. It is necessary to find out whether or not there is any serious injury, without unnecessary fuss. A minor graze or bruise can be left for treatment until after the lesson, the child being put back on the pony as soon as possible.

Although falls resulting in serious physical hurt are actually most uncommon during the course of the child rider's lessons, the instructor must know what to do should such a thing unfortunately occur. Indeed, instructors who hold qualifications from recognised organisations are nowadays required, by many of these organisations, to be certificated first-aiders and should treat any accident in accordance with current first-aid practices.

It is worth noting, however, that children do not always react to a fall in the same way as adults. For example, while immobility should be treated with caution it is, in children, often the result of combined winding and fright, in which case it usually rights itself within minutes. Stunned silence followed by loud crying is also usually the result of winding and fright, and the appalling roars of the child are quite an encouraging sign, as they rarely follow serious hurt. A child who is not significantly hurt should be calmed, and the work resumed as soon as possible.

However, even where no injury is apparent, the child's hat should be inspected for signs of obvious damage and the child carefully examined in the light of any which is detected. Also if the child wears spectacles it is necessary to check that they are in place and not damaged or, if they have fallen off, to see that they are not trodden upon.

A very good way of calming fright following a fall is to ask the child what happened, to convince him or her, if this is the case, that it was not the pony's fault, and to explain that the pony's feelings are hurt because the rider has fallen off through no fault of the pony. The child must therefore get back on and get going as soon as possible, so as to comfort the pony. (It is usually best from the point of view of the child's nerve to give the pony the benefit of the doubt in 'borderline' cases.)

On the other hand, if the fall plainly resulted from the pony's misbehaviour, fright can sometimes be calmed by rousing the child's pride on 'not letting him get away with that' lines.

It may be necessary for the instructor to ride the pony briefly to correct it for some misbehaviour if it is felt that the trouble will recur if the child is put back on immediately.

It is *not* a good idea to risk repeated falls, and if really necessary a different pony should be substituted or easier work undertaken, so that the lesson can be ended on a good note.

It is not necessary to remind the child of mishaps — unless they resulted from some plain disobedience or notable carelessness on the child's own part — but the instructor should remember them. Then, next time the same work is undertaken or a similar situation which led up to the fall arises, the instructor can make every endeavour to relieve any tension and get cheerfully past the moment.

CHAPTER 9

RIDING OUTSIDE

RIDING OUTSIDE the school is desirable to provide interest and variety, and the necessary practice in riding under different conditions. It encourages relaxation, self-reliance and the child's ability to manage the pony. It is a good plan to alternate lessons in the school with hacking out, during which a certain amount of instruction has to be given but the general atmosphere can be more informal than in a lesson in a confined space.

To a certain extent, riding outside in a field serves the same purpose, as the child riders are not so directly under the constant instruction which features in a manège lesson, and most ponies are more free-going and perhaps more cheeky than in the school.

Going out for a ride is enjoyed by most children, and is often chosen in preference to a school lesson if a choice is given to the younger and more inexperienced child. Both activities are necessary to the child's progress.

Taking out a ride of inexperienced children, not on leading reins, is quite exacting work for the instructor, because of the amount of supervision necessary, as outlined earlier. In my opinion at least one experienced helper is needed to accompany the instructor on escort work if more than two inexperienced children are taken out at a time. With a helper available the instructor can lead the ride and the helper, bringing up the rear, can see what is going on, warn the instructor if something goes wrong and help as necessary. Alternatively, the positions can be reversed with the helper leading the ride, so that the instructor is free to ride at the rear or move up and down the ride to give help and instruction as required.

If a considerable number of inexperienced children are out together it is a good plan to have more than one assistant – if possible enough so that, if need be, each experienced person can look after two children (one on each side).

Hacking, or 'going out', is very valuable in helping pupils to relax, in increasing their confidence and their ability to handle their ponies under different circumstances. Usually, it is also enjoyed as a change from 'lessons'. Here, the instructor has briefly halted the ride to point out something of interest in a nearby field. A helper is acting as rear escort.

It is often helpful for the instructor and each helper to carry two leading reins in their pockets, for use should the situation call for it.

Before setting out, thought needs to be given to the composition and order of the ride. It has to be decided, according to the district, traffic conditions and other circumstances, whether the ride is to go in single file or in pairs. If at all practical, I prefer to have the ride formed up in pairs, so that any pony of whose traffic manners *in all circumstances* one cannot be absolutely sure can be put inside another; so that ponies have company alongside and are then encouraged to keep up well; so that the children can talk to one another if they wish, encouraging relaxation; and so that the ride is not too long and difficult to supervise. If a ride in pairs is chosen it is necessary to instruct the children to form a single line if conditions require it, and it is helpful to arrange in advance (because of the common sense problem already outlined) which member of a pair is to go ahead and which drop behind if this is necessary, otherwise dithering will probably result.

Naturally, it is also sensible to arrange the order so that ponies which dislike each other are separated; those inclined to hot up if things get exciting are not at the back; the most inexperienced or nervous children are within easiest reach of the instructor or helper, and any other expedient is included which seems likely to make for the most orderly conduct of the ride when outside.

One of the most important precautions, if unnecessary difficulties are to be avoided, is to try to ensure that gaps do not occur in the ride, and the children must be urged to keep up and the pace regulated to allow for the slowest pony. It is annoying to have to keep waiting for ponies to close up, and usually lazy ones will slow to a walk or halt if the leader does so to allow them to catch up, leaving the gap still there. Gaps between ponies merely invite trouble because keen ponies are most likely to play up if finding themselves left behind and are tempted to put on a spurt to catch up, unbalancing their small riders at the most inconvenient moments.

In addition to setting a suitable pace, the instructor and helpers need, of course, to ride in such a way as to teach by example, and to display good manners when meeting traffic, other horses and pedestrians. Well-mannered, sensible, handy horses are essential for escort work. They allow the instructor and helpers to devote their attention to the ride and to anticipating anything likely to cause trouble so as to take any necessary action in good time, and so that ponies can be led from them, if this should become necessary.

The route taken needs to be planned carefully to suit the degree of experience of those on the ride. It is helpful if the children riding together are of roughly similar standard. If they are not, the route and tempo of the ride need to be geared to suit the least experienced. Interest can be added for the more experienced by the use of ingenuity in getting them to do something a little more exacting (such as riding with one hand for a spell, opening gates as required, and similar tasks) and by mounting them on ponies which require a little more skill to ride well.

With inexperienced children it is wise to canter in a confined area where, if necessary, the leader's horse can be manoeuvred as a buffer to prevent ponies passing it. An instructor escorting inexperienced children needs to acquire the ability (and the agility) to catch hold of the rein of any passing pony if one should get a bit over-enthusiastic (remembering, at the same time, to instruct the child to sit up!). Much trouble is avoided if ponies are not allowed to 'see too much daylight' when ridden out by small beginners.

As the children become more experienced, the rides can be varied by work in more open places where several can practise controlling their ponies abreast, by riding up and down inclines, along twisty paths, and by jumping small, easy gullies and fallen branches.

A lot of fun can be had as the children progress by such harmless games as singing in unison while cantering, pretending to be a troop of soldiers, or acting the part of a team of cowboys on a round-up.

Also, much can be taught about country lore, sensible riding behaviour and the care of ponies in various situations while riding out. The aim should be to make the rides as enjoyable and as much fun as possible, while retaining the supervision necessary for safety and the orderly conduct of the ride so as not to inconvenience others in any way.

The children's instructor needs to be prepared for the fact that at least with inexperienced and young children, it will be necessary to do quite a lot of work and expend a lot of care, skill, and probably also energy, when taking them outside. Frequent dismounting may be required to help in adjusting a girth, picking up dropped whips, rescuing possessions (or even small children – as mentioned elsewhere) from the branches of trees, and perhaps catch ponies who have lost their riders, while at the same time keeping control of the rest of the ride. This is another reason for the instructor choosing a sensible horse to ride (and preferably one which is not too tall!)

CHAPTER 10

ACTIVE RIDING

THERE IS, of course, no hard and fast dividing line between the passive and active stages in riding lessons – between, that is, the period during which the pupil learns to sit on the horse at all normal paces and also during any minor mishaps, and that in which the pupil learns to *control* the pony in normal circumstances, to anticipate and if possible forestall difficulties or to correct them when they occur. As outlined earlier, attempts should be made from the outset to encourage the child to exercise elementary control over the pony, and for a very long time after really active control has begun there will still be much to be taught and corrected about the position and aids in order to promote further efficiency.

There does come a time, however, during the course of the riding lessons, when the child is reasonably secure on the pony in normal circumstances, when it is necessary to gear the lessons more towards active control if progress and interest are to be maintained.

Riding outside encourages the child to control the pony, but in addition much of the school work in manège and/or field can be aimed at improving active riding and the use of intelligence as well as skill to achieve this.

Exercises

The carrying out of a number of simple school exercises and games is useful in this connection and also reduces the risk of boredom and adds a lot of interest and enjoyment to the lessons.

Each instructor can devise a great variety of these. A few are suggested here which I find helpful, by way of a guide to the possibilities.

A simple way to begin this work, encouraging control of the pony and also, to some extent, teaching a measure of judgement of pace and distance, is to mark out the manège with letters as in a dressage arena (or by such other method as may be convenient) and to use these letters for a number of simple exercises in control.

A start can be made by getting the children each to ride to a particular letter (looking where they want to go) and then halt. They can then be told to change places with one another – the rider at A taking his or her pony to stand where the rider at C is standing now, and vice versa. When this simple exercise has been carried out, several may be told to change places at once. It is important to instil the idea of always passing left-hand to left-hand when two ponies meet (unless otherwise instructed) if collisions are to be avoided. The work can be carried out first in walk and later, as progress continues, at other paces.

A development of this idea is to instruct the rear file in a ride to halt at a particular letter, wait until the ride is approaching from behind and then proceed round the school in front of the ride. This, too, can be carried out first in walk and later in trot or even, when the children have gained a good deal more experience, in canter. It helps to teach the child to control the pony and to judge how soon to begin preparation for walk and halt, when the ride is trotting, and how soon to walk on and, later, trot and canter in order to fit into the front of the ride without slowing it as it approaches or leaving a gap.

A further development is an exercise which I describe as 'spokes of the wheel'. In this, each member of the ride is instructed to halt at a particular marker, as the ride goes round the school, beginning from the rear. When all are halted at separate markers the children can be told to take note of their place and distance from the pony next in front of them. All are then told to walk on (and later, when able to carry out the exercise well, to trot or even canter on), trying to keep the same distances and looking across the manège for one another as they pass the markers. Simple enough on paper, this is quite a difficult exercise to do well, as keen ponies will try to close the gap and the slower ones need to be pushed on to keep their distances. At the end of the exercise, all can be warned in good time to halt at the marker at which they began the exercise, when the children need to use judgement to decide how soon to slow beforehand and can see clearly for themselves, because of their positions, whether or not they have carried out the exercise efficiently.

From work of this kind it is possible to move on to a variety of recognised school exercises such as turning across the school or circling by rides, rear files circling in the corners and taking the front of the ride, performing scissors movements, coming down the centre in half-sections (twos) and

There are many school exercises which are valuable in improving control and judgement of pace and distance. In this picture, two 'half-sections' (pairs) are about to join up to come down the centre of the manège in a 'section' (four abreast).

sections (fours), wheeling in sections, and a host of other similar manœuvres such as are carried out in military musical rides. All these exercises are most valuable in improving control and judgement of pace and distance, and are usually great fun and much enjoyed by classes of children when the progress of their lessons permits this work.

Games

Younger children usually enjoy games of follow-my-leader in which an older or more experienced child leading the ride carries out a variety of simple tasks on the move (such as riding with reins in one hand; sitting and then rising at the trot; removing and replacing a glove; quitting and crossing the stirrups; changing the stick from hand to hand; touching the toes, and so on) with the following children watching to spot the changes as carried out by the rider in front of them and then carrying them out themselves. As experience increases the children can take turns, as leading file, to set the exercises. At first, it is of course necessary to choose a sensible child to lead,

In a 'follow-my-leader' session, the leader carries out various simple movements – here placing a hand on the top of her hat – and those following copy the movements of the rider immediately in front of them.

A game of tag in progress, in which one child has a cloth tucked into the back of her collar and the others try to snatch it away.

and the leader must be told to use only exercises which can be carried out easily by the least experienced or secure child in the ride.

Periods of riding with a handkerchief under the seat without losing it, or with brown paper reins to encourage control with the minimum of pull on the reins are interesting for children and serve a useful purpose, in an enclosed school.

Games in which one child carries a handkerchief hanging from a pocket or collar, which the others try to remove – the successful 'pickpocket' then becoming 'it' – are useful, as are simple gymkhana events or even paddock polo (with a soft ball) or 'netball' played with a bean bag, if the facilities are available. Any games of this kind provide variety, encourage quick reactions, agility, ability to control the ponies and the independent use of different parts of the rider's body.

With all such games it is important to watch that the children do not become rough with the ponies and that excitement (of riders or ponies) is not allowed to develop to the point where small children become frightened or hurt, or where accidents occur. Very careful supervision is necessary and it is usually best if only short periods – as a part of the lesson – are devoted to games.

CHAPTER 11

STUDYING CHARACTER

IN ALL teaching it is most important, in my opinion, for the instructor to study the character and temperament of the pupil, so that the work can be arranged in such a way as to be most suitable for the individual. Learning to recognise, and trying to understand, the different temperaments of pupils is as important as studying their physical characteristics and problems, but is often a good deal more difficult. It requires sympathy, perception and a good deal of experience, but it is rewarding. This side of the instructor's work is often harder with children than with adults, because of the child's shyness, inexperience, and the difficulties of communication.

The child's temperament and degree of intelligence play a great part in the progress of his or her riding lessons. Nervous children require to be given confidence in their instructor, their pony and themselves. Lazy ones need stimulating. Children who are slow to grasp an idea need to have it demonstrated and explained clearly and patiently, often many times, before it sinks in. Quick, highly intelligent children readily become bored by too much repetition, while those who are slower can become bored by necessary work for which they have not understood the need.

Confidence Level

It is important to build self-confidence in children who lack this by providing ample opportunity in the lessons for them to do the kind of work which they find easiest and most enjoyable, and to introduce other work which they find difficult only gradually and for short periods.

An equally difficult problem to deal with is that of a swollen head! Some children who are progressing well and finding the work easy can suffer from this unattractive complaint to such an extent that they fail to try and reach a point at which it is hard to make further progress. These need to be taken down a peg. While it can sometimes be tempting to take a short cut to this by mounting them on a pony quite beyond their capabilities, the risk of accident or serious fright will prevent the conscientious instructor from doing this. Skilful planning is necessary to present such children with problems which will have the effect of showing that they have yet much to learn without risking any harmful consequences if they fail to surmount them. They need to be set tasks which will reveal their limitations to themselves and to their fellows in the class, while the less confident members of the ride have simpler things to do. If these tasks can be devised in such a way as to make it appear that all have equally difficult work to perform – although in fact this is not the case – so much the better.

One simple device which is quite useful in this respect is to mount the child on a pony which requires correct riding in order to go well into the corners of the manège. Another is to require periods of sitting trot on a pony upon which it is difficult to sit down well. A third is to require the child to lead the ride on a lazy pony, or one which is unwilling to leave its fellows. There are many similar instances of work which can be difficult, without risking injury to anything but pride.

Assertiveness

Attention has also to be given to the fundamental attitude of the child towards riding and towards the pony. Some children are natural leaders and will attempt from the outset to exert control, while others are hesitant and inclined to be passengers. Care has to be taken that the former do not become rough and every effort has to be made to get them to have some understanding of the animal and appreciation of its feelings. A number of children – more especially, but by no means entirely, boys – are inclined to regard a pony as they would a machine, and every effort has to be made to get them to appreciate the difference. Those who are hesitant in exerting control over the pony, on the other hand, need to be encouraged to be more dominant, and it is important that they should not be overfaced by having to deal too soon with self-willed, ungenerous ponies.

Many children, particularly the younger ones, can be easily put off by some seemingly trivial incident. If this happens (and it can sometimes be so marked as to cause refusal to jump, to canter, to go outside, or even to ride at all) a resourceful instructor, applying knowledge of the individual child, can help by providing some work in which the child is particularly interested. A few weeks of stable management only, for instance, with opportunities to watch other children ride (especially on a favourite pony or doing work which they most enjoyed when riding), often solves the problem.

Thought and Responsibility

In trying to teach children to be thinking riders, and to adopt a responsible attitude towards their ponies, it is most important to explain the reasons for doing things in a particular way, according to the age and understanding of the individual child. For example, in encouraging a child not to ride immediately behind another, it is usually much more effective to explain that one pony may tread on and hurt the heels of another, or be kicked, than to insist upon a certain distance between ponies merely as a matter of ride discipline. The need to halt exactly at a marker is more readily accepted if it is explained that this may not matter in a school, but would matter very much indeed at traffic lights outside. So long as the instructor has acquired a good knowledge of a child's thought processes and temperament, it will be possible to explain most instructions in this way, as and when necessary.

Speed of Learning

Since, for a combination of reasons, some children learn much more quickly than others, it is virtually impossible to say how long it will take any child to reach a certain point of progress.

In my experience small girls often learn more quickly – and appear to ride more intelligently – than small boys of the same age, up to about ten or twelve. Boys are in fact often considerably more nervous than girls in the early stages, but as they progress are inclined to become rough and to go through a stage in which they think of the horse as a kind of four-legged motor bike.

Some children are slow starters and take a very long time indeed to grasp each stage of the work, or to be able physically to carry it out. This is by no means cause for despair, as often these become extremely competent in the long run and the long periods of practice necessary at each stage, before moving on to the next, form an excellent foundation to ultimate good riding.

Almost all have spells in which, for no apparent reason, they seem to come to a halt in progress, and will remain at one stage for some time before suddenly taking a spurt, as it were, and resuming progress. This is particularly noticeable when the stage of more active riding is reached. Much patience is necessary and the instructor has to find ways to interest the child and to keep lessons enjoyable while one of these hiatus periods is being gone through.

Some individuals progress physically much more quickly than they do mentally, being able to carry out parts of the work well in a mechanical kind of way, without thoroughly grasping it with their intelligence. This is particularly true of younger children, but by no means confined to them. The instructor needs to be able to recognise this and to work gradually towards improving the child's understanding.

Others can understand clearly what is required and can recognise when something is being done correctly and when not, although they are unable physically to carry out much of the work. This is usually more easy to deal with than the reverse case, as physical exercises and practice are easier to arrange than work to improve understanding. It is important, however, not to be misled into pushing intelligent children too quickly into work of which they are not yet physically capable, or discouragement, strain and even accident may easily result.

The study of the individual child's temperament and progress is one of the most interesting aspects of the instructor's work. He or she needs to devise ways of slanting the lessons, so far as possible, to suit these. Although this is not easy to achieve when several children of differing temperaments are taught together, it is possible, by the use of much ingenuity, to go some way towards this. Efforts to do so can be most fascinating, and well worth while.

CHAPTER 12

FURTHER PROGRESS

IN THE earliest stages of riding, before the child has learnt body control and independent use of the limbs, 'aids' will, of necessity, have been decidedly primitive. Gradually, as the child gains in security, is able to maintain a fairly good position with independent use of the limbs, and can control the pony reasonably well, it becomes necessary for further progress to begin teaching some slightly more advanced work.

Establishing Contact

One of the most difficult things to teach is the maintenance of a proper contact with the pony's mouth and little progress in this direction is possible until a reasonably independent seat has been established. The most that could be hoped for during the early lessons is to teach the child not to use the reins for support, but to be able to use them with the minimum of roughness for simple steering, stopping and starting, in conjunction with the use of the legs and, as position in the saddle strengthens, the seat.

As position and security improve, efforts have to be made to begin to teach the rider to maintain a steady contact. This is something which, to a large extent, has to be learnt by practice. Most beginners have either no appreciable contact (with the reins more or less hanging in festoons); a very strong contact or pull; or, more commonly, a jerky contact with the reins becoming loose and tight by turns as the horse's head moves.

It is necessary to try to get the child to follow the movements of the pony's head with the hands or arms so as to maintain a proper constant contact, and in order to do this, the pupil must of course learn to get the horse to go forward from the legs and seat.

I try to explain what is necessary by likening the reins to elastic. I find it helps to hold one end of the reins while the child holds the other and to move the hands about to simulate the movements of the horse's head, with the child trying to follow the movements, keeping the 'elastic' taut but not tight.

A common error for the beginner attempting to follow the movements of the horse's head is to actively move the hands about, in a copy of the movements made by the horse's head, instead of allowing the head movement to move the hands. It is not at all easy to progress from the stage at which it is necessary to try to get the child to keep the hands as still as possible (instead of their jerking about with the movements of the rider's body) to that at which he or she is able to follow the movements and keep the hands still when necessary, in relation to the horse's mouth. A great deal of practice is necessary for this.

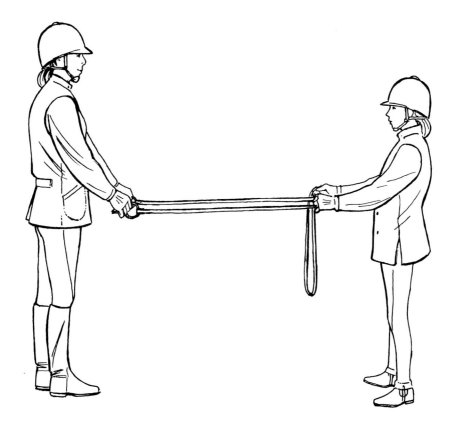

It helps to hold one end of the reins while the child holds the other, and to move one's hands to simulate the movements of the horse's head.

Developing Use of Aids

Teaching short turns is helpful in encouraging the rider to use the limbs independently to apply proper aids. It is usual to begin this work by teaching the turn on the forehand and progressing, when this has been learnt, to a turn, at the halt, on the haunches (this may be frowned upon nowadays from the point of view of dressage but it is a necessary preliminary from the rider's point of view to the demi-pirouette which is not readily understood unless the movement has been taught first from halt). In order to teach the child these movements it is necessary, naturally, to provide a pony which can and will turn more or less correctly in response to correct aids.

Common difficulties include the fact that in attempting to use one leg the child will be unable at first to keep from using the other, and will be unable to co-ordinate the use of the leg and hand, so that the pony is either pulled backwards or allowed to walk forwards during the turn. In addition, body position will be lost when the turn begins and the child has to be encouraged to think of sitting directly on top of a moving object and moving round with it, rather than staying still in one place despite the turn beneath.

In all slightly more advanced work it is especially necessary with children to try to ensure that they understand exactly what is required. Explanation and demonstration on a horse are helpful, of course. I have found that, particularly with younger children, demonstration by the instructor on foot – 'being a horse' – although perhaps slightly ridiculous to the onlooker, is also most helpful in getting the child to understand the movements which the pony is required to make. (In 'being a horse', the instructor's arms and legs perform the movements required from the horse's legs.)

When the child begins to attempt the movements explained, the instructor can help from the ground by encouraging the pony to move in the desired direction, so that the child gets some feel of the movement.

In demonstrating how the horse trots, preparatory to teaching recognition of diagonals and riding upon one or the other, it is helpful to tie a handkerchief round, or fit bandages or boots on, each leg of one pair of diagonals, so that they can be clearly seen when the horse is moving. Similarly in demonstrating the movements of canter it is helpful to fit a coloured rag or bandage on the leading leg, or one colour on the outside hind leg, another colour on the diagonal and a third on the inside foreleg, so that the child can be helped to follow the sequence. Here again, the instructor can help on foot by using his or her own arms and legs to show the sequence of movements.

Using brushing boots to demonstrate diagonals at the trot.

Using a brushing boot to demonstrate the leading leg at canter.

Turns, circles and, at a later stage, lateral work, are all useful for teaching the application of the aids. The work is similar to teaching the same movements to adults except that, with children, the instructor 'pretending to be a horse', definitely helps in getting the rider to picture the movement. This, of course, is in addition to explanation and mounted demonstration.

It is also helpful to get children to walk the required patterns and simulate the horse's movements themselves on foot, as this encourages them to identify physically and mentally with what is going on beneath them. In fact, I am by no means sure that this method would not be equally effective in teaching adults, were it not for the fact that it might meet with resistance from some pupils whose dignity would be offended. Fortunately this is not usually a problem with the child pupil.

Common Faults

Once the movements required have been grasped, a common fault is to attempt to obtain them by force. It takes a considerable time to convey the ideas of preparation and positioning for movements and of the aids as signals.

When the stage of somewhat more advanced work is reached, it is common for the rider to want to look down at the pony a great deal to see what is actually happening. Constant correction is necessary if this is not to become a habit difficult to eradicate. It takes a very considerable time for a rider to learn gradually to *feel* what is going on beneath the saddle. The instructor can help by 'counting legs' in trot, by explaining what is happening and encouraging the pupil to pay attention to the feel whilst being told what is actually going on at any given time. But only practice and repetition of the work will eventually solve this problem.

Explaining Impulsion

Perhaps one of the most difficult ideas to convey to children at this stage is that of impulsion, which almost invariably they equate with speed. Mounted demonstration is helpful; similes of a bouncing rubber ball or a compressed spring help to some extent to convey the idea. Neither of these is of use alone without some means of conveying the necessary feel. The instructor can help to some extent by providing situations in which the feel of impulsion is created artificially (such as by the child being told to slow the pony when some stimulus is encouraging it to go forward vigorously).

By the time the child has mastered the work already outlined and is ready to progress to learning about balance, collection and the work involved in trying to improve the pony, he or she has usually reached an age and/or standard when *for purposes of instruction* he or she can be treated as an adult. It is important to remember when this stage is reached, however, that a child cannot necessarily be expected to display the same sense of responsibility and resourcefulness at all times which might reasonably be shown by an adult at the same stage of riding. Children will display only as much responsibility in riding and handling horses (or, because of the excitement and 'difference' of riding, slightly less) than they would in other aspects of daily life.

CHAPTER 13

DEVELOPING THE CHILD RIDER

Outside Events and Self-reliance

WHEN THE child rider can exercise a reasonable degree of control in normal circumstances outside, the time has come to consider mounted participation in various outside events. Of course, dependent upon a child's temperament and interests, these may or may not appeal. Provided that a child who is not keen to undertake anything of this kind is not pressured into doing so, such activities are of considerable value to progress. They provide an extra interest and practice of a different kind from that in the usual lessons. They also help to increase self-confidence and self-reliance. Inevitably, children taught regularly in a riding school have to be subjected to a measure of supervision which is inclined to make them accustomed always to be told what to do.

It is an excellent thing for children to join the Pony Club. Those with their own ponies can attend mounted rallies and other events. Some riding schools are in a position to arrange for pupils to attend such rallies on school ponies, but even if this is not practical there are many visits and other functions which children without ponies can attend.

In many areas there are also plenty of small local shows and gymkhanas which have events suitable for fairly inexperienced children. If an opportunity can be given for competition in these they are enjoyed by many children. From the point of view of progress in the child's riding, it is desirable to approach these as a pleasant and interesting day out, at which success depends upon whether the pony has behaved nicely and been well controlled by the child, and both have enjoyed the outing. If some tangible result, such as a rosette, gets thrown in, too, this is a kind of bonus. If this type of atmosphere can be created by the person controlling the child's riding lessons, it is much more helpful than allowing the feeling to develop that it is of prime importance to win, which often leads to much disappointment and discouragement.

There are various other events, such as displays, parades and holiday courses, which can all add to interest and increase the child's experience of controlling ponies in company, which can be tackled as the child's increasing experience permits.

Since the object of encouraging children to take part in outside events (apart from adding variety and interest to their riding) is to increase practical experience and self-reliance, it is something of a problem to decide how much supervision needs to be given to the children when they attend them. Too much supervision defeats the object; too little can lead to accidents, or to children and ponies being a source of nuisance or worry to others.

Many riders have childhood recollections of having tackled quite cheerfully some pretty fearsome places on Pony Club paper chases, out hunting and the like – which some of us at least would think twice about in adult life – or having performed various other hair-raising feats more or less unwittingly. Such things are attributable to some extent to lack of adult experience of the possible pitfalls, leading to an unconcern sometimes wrongly mistaken for boldness or foolhardiness. Fortunately, the fearlessness of inexperience and their natural ebullience quite often allow children to get away with certain things with which an older person might not. The fact remains, however, that until children have acquired enough experience to recognise what can and cannot be sensibly attempted in riding, the responsibility to be able to cope with the unexpected, and a reasonable level of straightforward riding skill, a certain degree of supervision is necessary. This applies to the question of whether children should be allowed to hack out unaccompanied by an adult as well as to their attendance at organised events.

At Pony Club mounted rallies it is normal for the organisers to provide completely adequate supervision and (unless instructors or parents have some official part to play in the rally) children may, with confidence, be left in the care of those in charge – in fact, in my opinion, it is best for the child's own confidence to do this. The decision to be made, therefore, is whether to allow a child (who is permitted to ride unaccompanied near home) to hack on to the event and return home without adult supervision. This decision has to depend upon the age and experience of the child, the reliability of the pony, and the distance and type of journey to be covered. If quiet roads or tracks are involved and the child is experienced and can be trusted not to get into mischief on the way, this is normally suitable for older children (especially if they can go in company with others), and the experience is good for self-reliance.

In my opinion, children out hunting should always be supervised by an adult (except those old enough and experienced enough to be considered as adult), if only to prevent their inconveniencing others or causing damage through ignorance. Suitable supervision is, of course, provided by the organisers at special children's meets arranged for Pony Club branches.

It is not a good idea, in my view, for children (other than older, experienced teenagers) to attend horse shows or gymkhanas without adult supervision. The actual events in which they compete provide adequate opportunity for them to gain experience and develop self-reliance. Unsupervised children at local shows are tempted to use their ponies as grandstands, to ride them purposelessly and tiringly between events, and generally to make themselves a nuisance to others and to be a source of danger to themselves, their ponies and other people. Unfortunately, there is far too much of this kind of thing to be seen at small local events and unless children are supervised they may easily be led to copy such bad behaviour. Moreover, those not fully experienced in animal management need advice about whether and when to feed and water, the general care of the pony and themselves in heat or other adverse weather conditions, and all such matters.

It may therefore be practical to send sensible children to hack to and from a nearby show unsupervised, but a responsible adult ought, in my view, to be present on the showground to keep an eye on them as necessary throughout the length of their stay.

At all such outside events it is best to give the practical minimum of supervision and instruction, so that the children can look after themselves and their ponies to the greatest extent possible – but it is necessary that a responsible person should be on hand to supervise and to direct operations when necessary.

Other Aids to Learning

For older children in particular, the study of instructional books suitable to their age and the stage reached in their lessons is helpful, provided that this is of interest and pleasure to them and is not seen as a disliked homework chore.

Attending local shows gives sensible children the opportunity to practice self-reliance and take responsibility for their ponies.

As mentioned in Chapter 3, it is preferable if the instructor can recommend suitable books to the child's parents so that confusion is not caused by the introduction of ideas which are too advanced for the stage of riding reached. It is also best if the books suggested are in line with the teaching methods at the particular riding school attended, until such time as the child is sufficiently mature to compare and evaluate different ideas.

Further to this, it is helpful if the instructor encourages pupils to discuss any points in instructional books which may not have been understood. This part of the work can be extremely difficult if the books supplied are unsuitable for the pupil's age and standard of riding, as children tend to fasten upon some idea gleaned from a book and to pursue it, out of context, to their own confusion and the discomfiture of their teachers. This is an excellent reason for trying to ensure that the supply of books is suitable. Most young children who enjoy riding also enjoy fictional books with a horsy flavour.

When circumstances permit, riding lessons can be usefully supplemented by lectures. Lectures for children are best if they take the form of a lecture-demonstration, with the minimum of talk and the maximum of visual instruction. Various aspects of stable management and the handling of horses are examples of subjects taught effectively in this way, but lecture-demonstrations on various aspects of riding can also be most helpful.

Film shows suitable to the children's age and standard of riding are also helpful and usually enjoyed, as are visits to various places of horsy interest in the company of an experienced person who can explain what is going on if the child is unable to follow the proceedings. Lectures and shows of this kind can be followed up, if desired, by simple written tests on the subjects learnt, for older children.

Avoiding Boredom

Boredom is one of the most serious hindrances to progress in the teaching of children and the instructor needs to display continuous ingenuity if it is to be avoided. The introduction of games and small competitions into the lessons and rides, plenty of activity (and frequent changes of activity) as well as periods of rest from strenuous concentration, are helpful in preventing boredom. The provision of opportunities for question and discussion also help.

CHAPTER 14

SKILLS AND ATTRIBUTES OF THE CHILDREN'S INSTRUCTOR

TEACHING THE child rider is a somewhat specialised branch of riding instruction. There are some riders who are particularly gifted in making young horses, others whose particular skill lies in show jumping, in dressage or cross-country riding, and others who are all-rounders who could go to the top in any chosen branch of riding activity.

In the same way, some riding instructors have a particular gift for one branch of their work, while others are all-rounders in teaching riding. It does not follow that one instructor who achieves great success in some particular aspect of teaching will necessarily be especially suited to the instruction of children, or that another who gets excellent results in teaching children will be equally successful in some other type of instruction work. There are undoubtedly many, of course, who can teach equally successfully in a variety of ways. These people have great adaptability and can adopt different methods to suit whatever type of work is being undertaken.

One of the finest riding instructors it was ever my privilege to meet – an acknowledged expert, now, alas, no longer with us – was relatively unsuccessful with children and not only recognised this fact himself but stressed it. When he was once persuaded to take a special children's course, somewhat against his own better judgement, the results were notable for almost the entire class being quickly reduced to floods of tears and the instructor to frustration, embarrassment and firm declaration of 'never again'. He confessed himself scared stiff of facing a large class of children, unable to adopt a suitable approach to them and baffled by the whole business. Although this was doubtless a somewhat extreme case, it is clear that there are some people whose temperament, methods and attitude are particularly suited to teaching children, specifically, to ride.

As in any other comparable work, practice is of enormous help, but basic temperament fits some people especially for it.

Certain methods of teaching are particularly suited to children. They include provision for the general inexperience, physique and temperament of the young pupil, especially so far as gaining the pupil's confidence, maintaining interest and attention, and allowing for all aspects of physical and mental development are concerned. As already outlined, rather more supervision, and often more actual physical assistance, is required in teaching children, especially the younger ones, than is necessary for instructing adult novices.

Although it is a good idea to teach children recognised commands and terms so that they can understand them elsewhere in later riding life, the children's instructor can usefully adopt a highly individualistic style in explanation if necessary. There certainly has to be a preparedness to give simple explanations and clear demonstrations and to seek for ways to convey intended meaning clearly to the younger child. This requires adaptability and a willingness to experiment so as to find the best possible methods and approach for dealing with different individuals. It may also entail seeming slightly ridiculous in the eyes of the onlooker if this helps to achieve an objective.

I have vivid recollections of teaching children in a manège overlooked by a block of flats whose occupants were sometimes startled by my rear view on all fours demonstrating a turn, or the sight of me 'cantering' in slow motion on foot to try to show the sequence of the pace. I used to tell myself, when caught out in such undignified pursuits, that I was doing no possible harm to the flat-dwellers, was helping to make things easier for the child pupils, and if someone derived some amusement in the process, what did it matter? While the children's instructor must take seriously the responsibility of looking after and trying to teach children efficiently, it does not do to take oneself too seriously, I feel.

In my opinion, the instructor who wishes to make a success of teaching children needs first to like them and to be able to understand and communicate with them and win their confidence. Considerable patience, foresight and quick reactions are also essentials. While being fully responsible and able to maintain discipline, the instructor also needs a sense of proportion. A sense of humour and the ability to share in the fun and enjoyment of children are a great help, too.

The instructor, 'being a horse', is demonstrating on foot how the horse moves in right canter. The pupils' expressions indicate that this is an enjoyable and light-hearted way of putting across information, but their attention has been caught and they are likely to remember the lesson.

The children's instructor does not necessarily have to be a highly talented rider. Riding well enough to give clear, simple demonstrations; to put right ponies which have become indisciplined through being used for teaching novices; and to exercise good control with the minimum of effort when riding to escort hacks, is basically sufficient.

The instructor does, however, need to have plenty of horse sense (in both the literal and figurative senses of that expression) so as to be able to anticipate events and to exercise 'remote control' over the ponies being ridden by small beginners.

Teaching the child rider, for those suited to the work, is a most interesting, enjoyable and satisfying branch of riding instruction. It is

The instructor needs to be able to give clear, simple demonstrations. Here, the instructor has borrowed a pony from a member of the class to demonstrate a turn on the forehand.

certainly exacting, but the thought and effort required are more than repaid in the pleasure of sharing in the children's enjoyment, of watching their gradual journey on the road to becoming efficient riders and horsemasters, and of feeling that the basis is being formed for their progress in a pastime in which they can, if they wish, continue to take part throughout adult life.